SECRET
RHODE ISLAND

A Guide to the Weird, Wonderful, and Obscure

Robert Curley

Reedy Press
PO Box 5131
St. Louis, MO 63139
www.reedypress.com

No part of this publication may be reproduced or transmitted in any form or by
any means, electronic or mechanical, including photocopy, recording, or any
information storage and retrieval system, without permission in writing from the
publisher. Permissions may be sought directly from Reedy Press at the above
mailing address or via our website at www.reedypress.com.

Library of Congress Control Number: 2021950872

ISBN: 9781681063676

Design by Jill Halpin

Unless otherwise indicated, all photos are courtesy of the author
or in the public domain.

We (the publisher and the author) have done our best to provide the most accurate
information available when this book was completed. However, we make no
warranty, guarantee, or promise about the accuracy, completeness, or currency
of the information provided, and we expressly disclaim all warranties, express or
implied. Please note that attractions, company names, addresses, websites, and
phone numbers are subject to change or closure, and this is outside of our control.
We are not responsible for any loss, damage, injury, or inconvenience that may
occur due to the use of this book. When exploring new destinations, please do your
homework before you go. You are responsible for your own safety and health when
using this book.

Printed in the United States of America
23 24 25 26 27   5 4 3 2 1

To Christine, Shannon, Christopher, Laura, Shaina, and everyone else who delights in Rhode Island's weird and wonderful culture and history. And to Hazel, who I hope to introduce to Del's lemonade very soon.

Mohegan Bluffs

CONTENTS

ACKNOWLEDGMENTS

As always, thanks to my friends and family for their ideas and contributions to this book, including my fellow travelers Paul Kandarian, Gigi Mello, Christopher Rondina, Eric Therrien, and Grace Lentini. Also invaluable were the contributions of the Providence Warwick Convention and Visitors Bureau, the Blackstone Valley Tourism Council, the South County Tourism Council, Discover Newport, and the Block Island Tourism Council; the state's various local historical societies; and especially the historians and history buffs behind the Small State, Big History and ArtinRuins websites, Atlas Obscura, and the Greater Rhode Island Ruins and RI History Lost and Found groups. And of course to Seth MacFarlane for introducing the world to "Quahog, Rhode Island."

INTRODUCTION

Every state has its secrets, but Rhode Island has been accumulating mysteries longer than most. Right out of the gate, the Ocean State attracted more than its share of eccentrics and free spirits. The colony on Narragansett Bay got started in 1631 when founding father Roger Williams got the boot from Massachusetts for not being sufficiently puritanical, and in the centuries since, this small and unusually insular corner of New England has developed local quirks aplenty.

From an outsider's perspective, a book called *Secret Rhode Island* might almost seem redundant: blink on the drive up I-95 between New York and Boston and you might miss the state altogether. For those in the know, however, the fascinating tapestry of Rhode Island—woven through with Native American culture, the Industrial Revolution, immigration, revolution, hidden military bases, and a hundred other historic threads—includes a host of juicy legends and forgotten stories.

Monuments to chickens and potatoes, hermits and mall-squatting artists, underwater towns, hidden beaches, and tales of abandoned skyscrapers and railroad tunnels are just a few of the oddities uncovered in these pages. So pack up some hot wieners and coffee milk, throw on your *Family Guy* T-shirt, and join me as we stalk Rhode Island's most secret stories. You'll not only learn about the oddities of the Ocean State, but maybe also uncover a little history, gain some appreciation of Rhode Island's unique local culture—and discover why a tomato won't kill you, but macaroni just might.

MO' NUKES

What Charlestown nature preserve was the site of a fatal nuclear accident?

The 1,100-acre Francis T. Carter Preserve is one of the jewels of the Nature Conservancy's protected lands in Rhode Island—a place where you can hike or ride horses through a rare grassland habitat, paddle the Pawcatuck River, or scramble along paths tracing an ancient glacial moraine.

But this Charlestown property has a darker past: it was once the site of a secret processing plant for nuclear waste, where a Cold War accident claimed the life of a local worker from radiation poisoning. In July 1964, 37-year-old Robert Peabody triggered a nuclear explosion when he mistakenly emptied a concentrated uranium solution into a mixer. In a flash, Peabody was exposed to 10,000 rads of radiation—as much as the victims at Hiroshima. He died a few days later, becoming the first civilian victim of a nuclear accident in US history.

There's no remaining trace of the old United Nuclear Corporation facility (it shut down in the 1980s), although hikers may unwittingly retrace Peabody's last doomed steps as he staggered from the processing plant and collapsed. The tragedy largely has been forgotten, but Rhode Island's fling with the power of the atom has not. The Rhode Island Atomic Energy Commission has operated a tiny nuclear research reactor at

FRANCIS T. CARTER PRESERVE

WHAT: Nuclear accident site

WHERE: Francis T. Carter Preserve, 400 Old Mill Rd., Charlestown

COST: Free

PRO TIP: The 35-acre open area of the park isn't a natural meadow, but was clear-cut to provide habitat for grassland birds.

Top: *Grasslands at the Francis Carter Preserve*

Inset: *The former United Nuclear Corporation facility in Charlestown. (University of North Texas Libraries)*

the Bay Campus of the University of Rhode Island since the year of Peabody's death; the two-megawatt, water-cooled nuclear reactor is about a half hour away from the Carter Preserve—located on Reactor Way, of course.

The Francis Carter Preserve protects a mile-long stretch of the Pawcatuck River as well as an important piece of the Charlestown moraine, created by glaciers during the last Ice Age.

3

RAIL TALES

Where can you take a ride through a former trolley tunnel in Providence?

This is a tale of two tunnels—one open, one closed, and both on the East Side of Providence.

COLLEGE HILL TUNNEL AND EAST SIDE RAILROAD TUNNEL

WHAT: Historic East Side passageways

WHERE: Trolley tunnel entrance is at the corner of Waterman and N Main Streets; entrance to the railroad tunnel is in a parking lot behind the Providence Art Club, accessible from N Main St.

COST: RIPTA bus fare to ride through the trolley tunnel is $2

PRO TIP: The tracks running through the railroad tunnel once were carried to Union Station in downtown Providence via a viaduct. The train station still is there and houses offices and a brewery, but the viaduct has been demolished.

The College Hill Tunnel is far more accessible. Built in 1914, the tunnel burrows 2,000 feet from Thayer Street to North Main Street and originally was used by trolley cars, which previously struggled to mount the steep grade of College Hill (before the tunnel, the journey was aided by the only cable-car system built in New England, before or since).

The overhead wires and trolley cars are long vanished from the streets of Providence, but you can still ride through the tunnel on a city bus (routes 1, 32, 33, 34, 40, 49, and 61 go through the underground passage). Don't try to drive it, though—cars are prohibited.

Like the trolley tunnel, the East Side Railroad Tunnel runs under College Hill but is much longer—5,080 feet. Opened in 1908 to connect Union Station in downtown Providence to the Crook Point Bascule Bridge crossing the Seekonk River, the

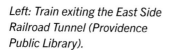

Left: Train exiting the East Side Railroad Tunnel (Providence Public Library).

Right: The entrance to the College Hill Tunnel.

Inset: The sealed entrance to the East Side Railroad Tunnel.

twin-tracked New York, New Haven & Hartford Railroad tunnel stretches from Gano Street to Benefit Street.

The last trains passed through the tunnel in 1981, and both ends have been sealed, but you can still see the old entry and exit portals, and the 22-foot-high, 30-foot-wide tunnel remains intact to this day. Although guarded by huge steel doors, the tunnel—with one set of tracks still inside—occasionally is breached by explorers and vandals, and the damp walls inside are marked with graffiti and other reminders of past visitors.

The East Side Railroad Tunnel remains closed, but the city of Providence is considering plans to convert the permanently open Crook Point Bascule Bridge into a public park.

BRIDGE TO THE FUTURE

How was a giant concrete bridge transformed into a charming, urban oasis?

Providence once held the *Guinness Book of World Records* distinction of having the world's widest bridge, but honestly, it was nothing much to brag about. Yes, the Crawford Street Bridge was wide—1,147 feet, to be exact. But it was a charmless steel-and-concrete slab whose main function, besides giving cars and pedestrians a dry way to cross from downtown to the East Side of Providence, was to cover up the smelly, polluted waters of the Providence River.

The tidal river had once been the lifeblood of the city, lined with warehouses and sailing ships in its heyday, but it slowly transformed into a murky dumping ground during the Industrial Revolution. In the 1980s, however, the river began rising again, thanks to an ambitious/improbable urban renewal project championed by Providence's then-mayor, the colorful (and twice-convicted) Salvatore "Buddy" Cianci.

Cianci and other city planners looked to Venice for inspiration for a reimagined downtown Providence with graceful arched bridges crossing its rivers, gondolas plying the waters, and a park surrounding a water basin on the site of the city's Great Salt Cove, which had been filled in the late 19th century.

CRAWFORD STREET BRIDGE

WHAT: World's (formerly) largest bridge

WHERE: Crawford Street Bridge, Providence

COST: Free

PRO TIP: The Providence River Pedestrian Bridge, opened in 2019, offers outstanding views of the elegant bridges that now span the river in downtown Providence.

Top: The Crawford Street Bridge, present day.

Left: Crawford Street Bridge, 1906.

The now normally proportioned Crawford Street Bridge is one of the several spans across the Providence and Woonasquatucket rivers that are part of Waterplace Park and the Providence Riverwalk. Completed in 1994, the park is home to Providence's popular WaterFire festival, and recently was linked shore-to-shore with a futuristic pedestrian bridge.

BURNSIDE'S SIDEBURNS

What general became more famous for his facial hair than his battlefield exploits?

Ambrose Burnside was nobody's idea of a military genius, but if battles were won not by arms but by hair, this Civil War general would have been a Napoleon.

Burnside, a resident of Newport and Bristol, fought in the Mexican–American War and on the western frontier before becoming a general during the US Civil War, where he suffered stinging defeats at the battles of Antietam and Fredericksburg. He isn't best remembered for that, however, or even for later becoming governor of Rhode Island and a US senator from the Ocean State.

Rather, Burnside's lasting fame derives from his distinctive muttonchops—a beard that plunged down from his temples and over his upper lip but left his chin unmolested. Originally called "burnsides," this distinctive style of facial hair later was reversed into "sideburns" and applied generally to hairstyles that creep down from the scalp onto the cheeks—accompanying mustache or no.

You can visit Burnside's grave in Providence's Swan Point Cemetery, but to get a fuller appreciation of the glorious side whiskers that inspired everyone from Joe Namath and Clyde

BURNSIDE PARK

WHAT: Ambrose Burnside statue

WHERE: Burnside Park, Providence

COST: Free

PRO TIP: Burnside's Providence home still stands: the Burnside House, with its distinctive semicircular tower and porch, is located at the corner of Planet and Benefit Streets.

General Ambrose Burnside

Frasier to Vegas-era Elvis and the Wolverine, check out the bronze statue of a mounted Burnside by Launt Thompson at the heart of Burnside Park in downtown Providence, across from City Hall.

STALAG SOUTH COUNTY

Where were German POWs taught how not to be Nazis?

Fort Kearney was built as part of the coastal defense system protecting Narragansett Bay prior to World War I, but by the second world war its gun emplacements had been declared obsolete and the military installation was slated for decommissioning.

But Fort Kearney's service wasn't over yet. In 1945, as World War II wound down, the 20-acre coastal fort (now the Bay Campus of the University of Rhode Island or URI) in Narragansett was transformed into a prisoner-of-war (POW) camp. The camp had a very specific mission: to turn German prisoners away from Nazi ideology and instill the democratic norms that would be needed in Germany after the war.

Championed by Eleanor Roosevelt, the Special Projects Division of the US Army established the camp and tasked its inmates to produce *Der Ruf* (The Call), a German-language newspaper championing American values that was distributed to the 140 German prisoner-of-war camps throughout the US.

URI BAY CAMPUS

WHAT: Former German POW camp

WHERE: URI Bay Campus, 215 S Ferry Rd., Narragansett

COST: Free

PRO TIP: Some of the coastal defenses at Ft. Kearney still are visible: URI's nuclear reactor was built on top of a former gun emplacement, for example.

The URI Bay Campus is home to the school's Graduate School of Oceanography and the *Narragansett Dawn*, one of the world's premier oceanographic research ships.

Top: Former gun emplacement at Fort Kearney

Inset: Der Ruf *newspaper*

The specially selected camp inmates also screened movies and books to determine if they were suitable for viewing and reading by German prisoners.

After the war, some of the editors of *Der Ruf* continued publishing the newspaper in Germany, promoting democracy but also criticizing the US occupation of Germany.

Fort Kearney prisoners were lightly guarded and even allowed excursions to nearby Narragansett Beach, and no escape attempts were ever reported. German POWs also were held on Dutch Island and at Fort Getty in Jamestown, which also provided reeducation classes to inmates.

SHOPPING SHAFTS

Is there a coal mine under one of Rhode Island's most upscale shopping centers?

The Garden City Center in Cranston is acclaimed as Rhode Island's premier open-air shopping destination, filled with fashion shops like J. Jill, Talbots, and Lululemon, fine dining at Avvio, and home decor and housewares from Crate & Barrel, Pottery Barn, and Williams-Sonoma.

Turn back the clock to the 1950s, however, and the scene would have been quite different, with soot-covered miners plunging deep into the earth to pull anthracite coal from a seam 130 feet down. Above ground, a processing plant prepared the low-quality coal into usable fuel.

GARDEN CITY CENTER

WHAT: Site of the Budlong Coal Mine

WHERE: Garden City Center, 100 Midway Rd., Cranston

COST: Free

PRO TIP: Coal was first mined in Rhode Island in 1808, and mines were once located in Portsmouth, Cumberland, and Providence.

The Cranston (Budlong) Coal Mine remained active from 1866 until 1959, when a cave-in resulted in the death of a miner and the operation finally was shut down. Construction of the shopping center had begun even before the mine's demise, and by the 1960s Garden City Center was in its full glory, even playing host to the Miss Rhode Island Universe competition.

The entrance to the Budlong Coal Mine was approximately where the Newport Creamery restaurant and ice cream parlor stands today.

Top: Budlong Coal Mine (Providence Public Library)

Inset: Garden City Center

Lurking below the landmark gazebo in the parking lot, however, are traces of the old mineshafts: a 50-foot-deep hole opened up during construction a few years back, for example. Other than that the only digging going on in Garden City is for money to spend at the retail shops, but Roger Williams Park Museum has examples of coal extracted from the Cranston Coal Mine.

LOST ISLAND

What happened to the island off the coast of Warwick purchased from the Narragansett sachem Miantonomi in 1642?

It's not exactly Atlantis, but Greene Island in Narragansett Bay—once 14 acres of bluffs, woodlands, and farmers' fields—has almost entirely vanished beneath the waves, the victim of storms, erosion, and rising tides.

You'll still find Greene Island on maps, sitting just outside Occupaspatuxet Cove in Warwick, and someone is still paying taxes on the 8.5 acres of the island that supposedly still remain. But if you try to visit, the best you can expect to find is a shallow sand flat exposed at low tide, with the bones of an old shipwreck the sole remaining occupant.

The island—named for Warwick cofounder Capt. John Greene, who bought the land from Miantonomi—actually has been shrinking since the 19th century. Even into the 1920s, it had trees, freshwater springs, and sandy bluffs that were popular terrain for local motorcycle riders, who could reach the island via a sandbar. Earlier, there had been cornfields on the island, and locals would visit to camp and fish for crabs and rake for clams on its shores.

No houses were ever built on Greene Island, although in the early 20th century some drifters lived on barges abandoned on its shores. The beginning of the end for Greene Island was the great hurricane of 1938, which tore the island in half. In

GREENE ISLAND

WHAT: Vanishing island in Narragansett Bay

WHERE: Off Gaspee Pt. in Warwick

COST: Free

PRO TIP: Unless you have a boat, the easiest place to get a glimpse of Greene Island at low tide is from the beach at the end of Rock Ave. in Warwick, where there's a public shoreline access point.

Remains of sunken ship on Greene Island (Greater Rhode Island Roaming)

recent decades, residents have seen the bedraggled island slowly diminish from an eelgrass-covered speck of land off Gaspee Point to almost nothing but a memory.

The Narragansetts called the cove where Greene Island is/was located *Occupaspatuxet*, which means "meadows cut through by a river."

TARA NORTH

Did Rhode Island once have slave plantations?

One of the curiosities about Rhode Island is how the smallest state ended up with the longest official name in the country. From colonial times until 2020, the official name was the State of Rhode Island and Providence Plantations, and therein lies a dark story about the state's founding.

The Providence Plantations (later Rhode Island) were founded by Roger Williams in 1636, and while the colony was considered a bastion of religious freedom compared to the Puritan-led Massachusetts Bay Colony, slavery was legal in Rhode Island from its founding until gradual emancipation was written into law in 1784.

During the colonial period, Rhode Island had the highest percentage of enslaved persons in its population of any state in New England. And while historically the word "plantation" was used synonymously with "colony," Rhode Island did in fact have large farms with fields worked by slaves. These unwilling workers included enslaved Native Americans and, later, Africans brought to America via the Triangle Trade, which was facilitated largely by wealthy merchants from Rhode Island. The Triangle Trade involved the transatlantic sale of slaves, rum, molasses, and other goods between the West Indies, Africa, and New England.

Hannah Robinson Tower at the corner of US Route 1 (Tower Hill Road) and Route 138 (Bridgetown Road) commemorates the tragic love affair of the daughter of Rowland and Anstis Robinson.

Rowland Robinson House

Large landowners collectively known as the Narragansett Planters, for example, ran slave plantations in South County right up through the Revolutionary War. And though they're not labeled as such, you can see old plantation houses in Rhode Island just as you can tour antebellum mansions in the South. The Rowland Robinson house in Saunderstown is one example, and Smith's Castle—now a museum house in North Kingstown—is another. The latter is the oldest slave plantation house in the United States.

WHAT: Rhode Island plantation houses

WHERE: Rowland Robinson House, 450 Old Boston Neck Rd., and Smith's Castle, 55 Richard Smith Dr., North Kingstown

COST: Smith's Castle entry fee is $10 for adults, $5 for children. The Rowland Robinson House is a private home.

PRO TIP: *The Economic Activities of the Narragansett Planters*, a 1939 mural by Ernest Hamlin Baker that depicts slavery in Rhode Island, hung for many years in the Wakefield Post Office and now is on display at the South County History Center in Kingston.

STRANGE ENDEAVOR

How did Australia's most famous ship end up on the bottom of Newport Harbor?

When Lieutenant James Cook of the Royal Navy set out to explore the South Pacific in 1768, he surely never imagined that his trusty bark HMS *Endeavour* would come to an ignominious end in Rhode Island less than a decade later.

Originally launched as a coal ship before being commissioned into the Royal Navy, the 97-foot sailing vessel carried Cook and 85 crewmates from Plymouth around Cape Horn and to Tahiti, where the scientific research vessel and crew were tasked with observing the transit of Venus across the sun. Cook then steered toward uncharted waters to the south in search of a presumed undiscovered continent in the southern sea, known at the time as Terra Australis Incognita, or the unknown land of the south.

Cook proved the legend of the lost continent real in April 1770, when he sailed *Endeavour* into Botany Bay in what is now the heart of the metropolis of Sydney, Australia. The *Endeavour* and her crew would survive running aground on the Great Barrier Reef and the long journey back to report Cook's discovery to England in July of 1771.

Cook was hailed as a hero, but the *Endeavour* received no such glory. The bark was repurposed as the troop ship *Lord Sandwich*, which, in 1775, took her to Newport as part of an effort to bolster occupying British forces in anticipation of a French-American effort to retake the port city. Fearing an attack by the French Navy, the British decided to block Narragansett Bay by scuttling a number of surplus ships, including the *Lord Sandwich*. And there this great vessel of exploration lay, undisturbed, until marine archaeologists identified a wreck believed to be Cook's famous ship in 2018.

Left: Ship painting HMS Endeavour *off New Holland by Samuel Atkins (National Library of Australia)*

Right: Plaque on Goat Island identifying the location of shipwrecks in Newport Harbor

Newport visitors can experience many sites associated with the occupation of Newport, including the Old Colony House where local leaders surrendered the city to the British. But if you want to see the HMS *Endeavour*, the closest you'll get is a visit to the full-scale replica sitting at anchor in Botany Bay in Sydney.

NEWPORT HARBOR

WHAT: Wreck of the HMS *Endeavour*

WHERE: Newport Harbor

COST: Free

PRO TIP: HMS *Resolution*, Cook's flagship on his second circumnavigation of the globe in 1772 to 1775, also may be one of the wrecks at the bottom of Newport Harbor.

YO HO, OH NO

Where were 26 pirates sent to the gallows in Newport?

The largest mass execution of pirates in the American colonies took place in Newport in 1723—a public event that was loudly cheered despite the city's reputation as a pirate's haven.

The pirates—Captain Charles Harris and crewmembers of the sloop *Ranger*—had been captured off Block Island after a battle with the British man-of-war *The Greyhound*. Accused of plundering ships along the East Coast and committing atrocities against the crews of captured vessels, the pirates quickly were convicted and condemned to hang during a two-day trial in Newport.

The execution on July 19, 1723, was "attended by a vast multitude from every part of New England," according to an account of the hanging written in 1843. The gallows, adorned with the pirate flag taken from the *Ranger*, was set up on Newport's Bull's Point, aka Gravelly Point, and after the execution all of the men were buried on the north shore of Goat Island between the low- and high-tide mark.

GOAT ISLAND

WHAT: Pirate mass hanging and grave site

WHERE: Goat Island, Newport

COST: Free

PRO TIP: Newport Craft Brewing & Distilling named its Thomas Tew rum after a Newport-born buccaneer known historically as "the Rhode Island Pirate."

Charles Harris's infamous partner in piracy, Edward Low—one of the most brutal and sadistic of the pirates of the Caribbean—escaped justice in Newport by eluding the British warship that captured Harris and his men.

Top: Lighthouse on Goat Island, where 26 pirates were buried after being hung on nearby Gravelly Point.

Inset: Pirate flag flown by Charles Harris (RootofAllLight)

In later years the cove around Gravelly Point was filled, obliterating the execution site near the end of Long Wharf, but the pirates are thought to have been buried near the present location of the Goat Island Lighthouse.

CLASSICAL GAS

How did Pelham Street in Newport become the first street in the US to be illuminated by gaslight?

"Gaslighting" didn't always have a negative connotation: back in the 19th century, when most homes and streets were lit by whale oil or candles, gas lamps were a technological wonder. Newport resident David Melville made his living as a pewterer, but as a sideline designed a system for lighting his Pelham Street home in 1805–06 with hydrogenous gas, derived from burning coal and wood.

That alone was well ahead of its time—the first residential gas company in Newport wouldn't be established for another half century—but what truly put Melville's name in lights was the addition of a gas-powered streetlamp outside his front door. It was the first gas streetlamp in America, predating Baltimore's famous municipal street-lighting project by more than a decade.

Melville filed the first patent for gas lighting in the US, and although he never got rich off of the technology, his accomplishment is noted with a plaque on Pelham Street. You can visit the site of the country's first gas streetlight day or night, because Pelham Street is lit to this day by gaslight. Several other

PELHAM STREET

WHAT: First gaslit street in America

WHERE: Pelham St. side of the One Pelham East nightclub, 270 Thames St., Newport

COST: Free

PRO TIP: One Pelham East is one of Newport's top live music venues and home to the city's only dueling piano bar.

Newport also claims to be the first place a photograph was taken by electric light, in 1866.

Pelham Street gas lamp

Newport streets also have their colonial charm enhanced by gas lamps, and if you really want to embrace the theme on a Newport visit, the Gas Lamp Grille serves up everything from tacos to lobster just two blocks away, on Thames Street.

WELCOME CONE

Why is there a giant pine cone dangling over Federal Hill?

One of Rhode Island's most enduring myths is that there's a pineapple hanging from the gateway arch over Federal Hill, Providence's lively Little Italy. But while the pineapple is indeed a traditional symbol of hospitality, and Federal Hill is one of the state's top culinary destinations, it's actually not a tropical fruit but a pine cone that welcomes people to the hill.

The biggest clue to this can be found in the name of the bronze sculpture hung from the arch when it was raised in 1981: *La Pigna*, which is Italian for pine cone. Designed by Albert Veri Associates, the arch and *La Pigna* were part of a Federal Hill urban renewal project. The sculpture drew inspiration from classic Italian designs, notably the Fontana della Pigna, a fountain installed in Rome in the first century AD near the Pantheon, and still displayed on the wall of the Vatican facing the *Cortile della Pigna*, or Pine Cone Courtyard.

FEDERAL HILL ARCH

WHAT: Italian pine cone symbol of welcome

WHERE: Atwells Ave., Providence

COST: Free

PRO TIP: The red, green, and white stripes painted down the middle of Atwells Ave. signify Federal Hill's Italian heritage and guide the procession in the annual Feast of St. Joseph parade.

There's a second symbolic pine cone on Federal Hill that's also sometimes overlooked: it adorns the top of the decorative fountain at the center of DePasquale Square, the cultural center of the neighborhood.

Rhode Islanders and Federal Hill visitors will surely continue the "pineapple or pine cone" debate. In fact, if you order the

The Federal Hill Arch

Arch cocktail at Rhode Island's Siena restaurant, you'll get a vodka martini shaken with pineapple juice—definitely more tasty than a pine cone cocktail, historically accurate or not.

The name Federal Hill dates back to 1788, when a celebration was held in honor of the ratification of the US federal Constitution, which Rhode Island was actually the last state to sign off on, in 1790.

LOOK, UP IN THE SKY . . .

Why is the most iconic building on the Providence skyline called the Superman Building?

The 428-foot art deco skyscraper at 111 Westminster Street is Providence's tallest building and was born as the Industrial National Bank Building when it opened in 1928. Nobody calls it that, however. To nearly every Rhode Islander, it's simply the Superman Building, a nod to the limestone-clad office tower's resemblance to the tall building that Superman "leaps in a single bound" in the early *Superman* comics and TV series.

In truth, the Daily Planet building that the superhero soars over was based on the former Toronto Star building in Toronto, and the building shown in the TV series is Los Angeles City Hall. So the only thing actually soaring above Providence's Superman Building are the peregrine falcons nesting on the 26th floor.

However, a plotting meeting by Superman's archnemesis, business magnate Lex Luthor, would have been right at home on the building's 29th floor, which has an ornate meeting room designed after a gondola of *Her Majesty's Airship No.1*, the first dirigible commissioned into the Royal Navy. It would take a heroic effort to see this unique space high above Providence, however. The Gondola Room, like the rest of the Superman Building, has been vacant and closed to the public since 2013, but a renovation project is in the works.

INDUSTRIAL NATIONAL BANK BUILDING

WHAT: The Superman Building

WHERE: 111 Westminster St., Providence

COST: Free

PRO TIP: The Superman Building is the focal point of artist Shepard Fairey's *Providence Industrial* mural, painted on the northwest side of the Pell Chaffee Performance Center, home of Trinity Repertory Company.

The "Superman" building

MIGHTY 'MITE

Why is there a giant termite hovering over Interstate 95 in Providence?

To the untrained eye, Providence's Big Blue Bug looks like a grasshopper, but any exterminator worthy of wielding a pesticide jug will tell you that this intimidating insect is a winged adult *reticulitermes flavipes*, or the dreaded, house-eating eastern subterranean termite.

The Big Blue Bug was born in 1980 as a marketing gimmick for New England Pest Control, which spent $20,000 to mount the 58-foot-long, nine-foot-tall, 4,000-pound steel-and-fiberglass termite on the roof of its building. It was originally painted purple, but quickly faded to blue in the sun. After a local traffic reporter dubbed it the Big Blue Bug, the nickname stuck, even after a contest gave the bug the official name "Nibbles Woodaway."

The bug became an instant landmark and Rhode Island cultural icon, thanks to its premier location, viewed by thousands of commuters daily on the busy Interstate 95 corridor. It has starred in the *Family Guy* series and the *Dumb and Dumber* movies, and gets dressed up for the holidays each year: colored lights for Christmas; a red, white, and blue top hat for Independence Day; and—while some would say something 928 times the size of a real termite needs no other costume—a witch's hat for Halloween.

THE BIG BLUE BUG

WHAT: Giant insect statue

WHERE: 161 O'Connell St., Providence

COST: Free

PRO TIP: Rhode Island has an official state insect, but it's not a termite: the honor goes to the American Burying Beetle, best known for making its home in the bodies of dead animals.

The Big Blue Bug with its Christmas "Rudolph" nose attached

Perhaps bowing to the inevitable, New England Pest Control changed its name to Big Blue Bug Solutions in 2012.

ROLLING TO VICTORY

Did Rhode Island once rule the NFL?

Rhode Island has produced a handful of football stars over the years, including kicker Al Del Greco and Super Bowl winner and two-time All Pro defensive end Gerry Philbin; the state even hosted training camp for the New England Patriots at Bryant University for many years. But the Ocean State is hardly known as a football powerhouse, which is why it's a surprise to learn that a National Football League team from Providence once was the top gang on the gridiron.

The Providence Steam Roller played in the NFL from 1925 to 1931, with home games taking place at the 10,000-seat Cycledrome, a stadium built primarily for bicycle racing located off North Main Street (currently the site of an Ocean State Job Lot store). Thanks to the odd dimensions of the Cycledrome, games were played on a field with one end zone that was 10 yards wide and another that was just five yards wide.

PROVIDENCE STEAM ROLLER

WHAT: Rhode Island's NFL Championship team

WHERE: 50 Ann Mary St., Pawtucket

COST: Free

PRO TIP: Providence is more convenient to Gillette Stadium than Boston, so the six-time NFL champion New England Patriots park their team plane at T. F. Green Airport, and visiting teams usually stay in Providence hotels.

Pawtucket resident and defensive tackle Gerry Philbin was a member of the 1968 Jets team that defeated fellow Rhode Islander Tom Mitchell and the Baltimore Colts in Super Bowl III.

*Top: Football at the Providence Cyclodrome
(Providence Public Library)*

*Inset: Ticket stub to Providence Steam
Roller game vs. the Green Bay Packers*

During the team's brief time in the league, the Steam Roller hosted the first night game in NFL history (using a white ball to aid visibility), and Brown University alumnus Fritz Pollard, the NFL's first Black head coach, was among the players who suited up in the Steam Roller's red-and-white jerseys emblazoned with the image of a husky dog.

By far the team's shining moment of glory came in 1928, however, when the Steam Roller finished the regular season with a record of 8–1–2 and earning the title of NFL Champions, which is those days was based on percentage of wins, not a playoff system. The most recent now-defunct team to win the NFL title, the Steam Roller later inspired the name of the Providence Steamrollers basketball team, which played 1946 to 1949 and were one of the 11 original NBA franchises.

LITTLE HIGH POINT

What "peak" in Rhode Island was considered the hardest to conquer by mountain climbers?

Nobody ever got a nosebleed trying to summit Rhode Island's modest hills, which don't even remotely qualify for the title of "mountains." Jerimoth Hill, at a mighty 812 feet above sea level, is the highest point in the state. Yet for years it proved to be an unattainable conquest for climbers and hikers seeking to stand on every high point in the US.

As you might guess, climbers who had stood atop 20,310-foot Denali in Alaska weren't exactly intimidated by the comparative speed bump of Jerimoth Hill. The problem was one of access. Whereas most other high points are in parks, Jerimoth Hill, in the town of Foster, is surrounded by private property.

So, while the peak itself is owned by Brown University, which occasionally uses the cleared summit as an astronomical observatory, the access path from nearby State Route 101 crosses the driveway of a local property owner who once zealously protected his land from intruders. Mountaineers who literally had to brave minus-40-degree temperatures and a two-week journey to reach the top of Denali were thwarted less than a third of a mile from the high point of little Rhode Island.

JERIMOTH HILL

WHAT: Rhode Island's highest point

WHERE: Look for the brown Jerimoth Hill sign on the south side of Rte. 201, east of Pole 212.

COST: Free

PRO TIP: Summit pictures atop Jerimoth Hill basically consist of standing on a big glacial boulder, although there is an official US Coast and Geodetic Survey marker on the state's highest point.

High point marker and
Jerimoth Hill trail sign

The unwelcoming property owner died in 2005, however, and the access path eventually ended up in the hands of the state. Today, the 0.3-mile trail to the summit from Route 101 is an officially designated hiking trail, and highpointers easily can acquire their selfies at the summit.

The elevation gain from the trailhead to the summit of Jerimoth Hill is a mere 10 feet—about the same as climbing a flight of stairs in a typical home.

33

RED ROYALTY

Why does Rhode Island have a monument to a chicken?

With all due respect to Foghorn Leghorn, there's no more famous chicken in the world than Rhode Island's state bird, the Rhode Island Red. Originally bred by William Tripp and Isaac Champlin Wilbour of Little Compton from several varieties of Asian chickens, these distinctively colored fowl were introduced in 1854 and quickly became popular for both their flavorful meat and prodigious egg-laying ability. Thanks to the Rhode Island Red, Little Compton had a brief but glorious run as the poultry capital of the US in the 19th century.

If you buy eggs from a Rhode Island farm, they're likely to be brown and laid by a Rhode Island Red hen. Docile, beautiful, and productive, the Rhode Island Red also is a favorite of backyard farmers. It remains one of the most common breeds of chicken, and can be found everywhere from New England to the Caribbean and beyond.

In 1925, the Rhode Island Red Club of America (yes, such a thing existed) erected a monument to the Rhode Island Red in

RED ISLAND RED MONUMENT

WHAT: Homage to a famous chicken breed

WHERE: Intersection of Main St., Adamsville Rd., and Old Harbor Rd., Little Compton

COST: Free

PRO TIP: Eggs from Rhode Island Red chickens are on the menu at the Barn restaurant, across the street from the monument and one of the state's top breakfast joints.

The Rhode Island Red is considered the top breed for backyard chicken breeders. Hens lay 200–250 eggs annually.

Rhode Island Red monument in Adamsville

Adamsville, complete with a bas relief of a regal red hen. Sculpted in bronze by Henry L. Norton, the monument stands at the intersection of Main Street, Adamsville Road, and Old Harbor Road. In 1954, a second plaque was added near the Tripp farm in Little Compton to mark the 100th anniversary of the breed.

SOLDIER SNATCHING

Where did a British general get caught in his underwear during the Revolutionary War?

December 12, 1776, was one of the darkest days for George Washington's Continental Army, because a British reconnaissance party captured Major General Charles Lee, Washington's second-in-command, in a New Jersey tavern. However, a Providence hatter-turned-soldier, Lieutenant Colonel William Barton, would soon play a key role in avenging the embarrassing incident and winning Lee's freedom.

Spies had told Barton, who commanded colonial troops in Tiverton, that General Richard Prescott, who led the 3,000 British troops occupying Newport, was spending his nights at a lightly guarded farmhouse in Middletown. Barton devised a plot to kidnap Prescott, who as a prisoner of war could then be exchanged for Lee.

On the moonless night of July 10, 1777, Barton led a raiding party of 48 men that crossed Narragansett Bay by whaleboat, snuck behind enemy lines, and stormed the home of Quaker farmer John Overing, where Prescott was sleeping.

PRESCOTT FARM

WHAT: Kidnapping of a British general

WHERE: 2009 W Main Rd., Middletown

COST: Free

PRO TIP: Also on the Prescott Farm property is a unique windmill with two sets of grinding stones, once used as part of a whiskey distillery.

Despite his humiliating capture, Colonel Prescott was promoted to major general in 1777 and lieutenant general in 1782.

Left: General Richard Prescott

Right: Prescott Farm (Newport Restoration Foundation)

The raiders quickly disarmed the lone sentry on duty and captured Prescott and his aide de camp, both in various stages of undress. The prisoners were hustled back to the whaleboats and rowed back to the mainland right under the guns of the British fleet, the task force slipping away with its prize despite the alarms being raised back on Aquidneck Island.

The hoped-for prisoner exchange between Lee and Prescott took place in 1778. Barton's raid was hailed for its audacious success, a real morale boost for the rebel side. Tiverton's Fort Barton, named for the daring colonel, is a Revolutionary War earthwork close to the spot where Barton launched his raid. Prescott Farm in Middletown—named for the kidnapped general, not that he'd probably appreciate the honor—includes the Overing House and a British guard shack dating from the occupation of Newport.

HISTORIC ROOTS

Did a tree really eat the body of Rhode Island founder Roger Williams?

When Rhode Island founder and preacher Roger Williams died in 1683 at age 79, he was buried in a family plot in the backyard of his family home in Providence. But historic preservation wasn't a big thing back in those days, and when Williams's old house collapsed about half a century later, the grave site largely was forgotten.

That is until 1860, when a group seeking to honor Williams decided to excavate his final resting place and give him a burial worthy of the state's founding father. To their surprise, the dig yielded no intact bones, but instead an arboreal curiosity: an apple tree root seemed to have traced the outline of Williams's body, including bends corresponding to his legs, knees, and feet.

Thus was born the legend of the tree that ate Roger Williams.

The few human remains found in the grave (mostly teeth and bone fragments) were reinterred in a tomb under a monumental statue of Williams at Prospect Terrace on Providence's East Side. The "Williams Root" also was preserved in a place of honor, enclosed in an appropriately coffin-shaped display case

JOHN BROWN HOUSE MUSEUM

WHAT: Preacher-eating tree

WHERE: John Brown House Museum, 52 Power St., Providence

COST: Museum admission is $10 for adults, $6 for children

PRO TIP: The John Brown House has been praised for its opulence for centuries, but it has at least one quirky oddity: a statue of a gray squirrel posed prominently over a fireplace mantel. Nicknamed Misha, the squirrel also is incorporated into the logo of the Rhode Island Historical Society.

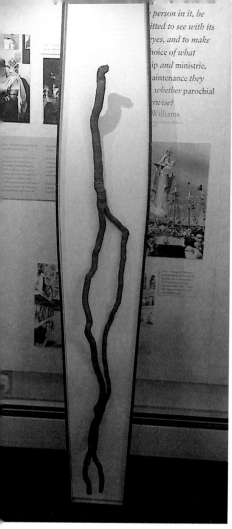

Left: The Williams Root (Roger Williams National Monument/National Park Service)

Right: The Banishment of Roger Williams *(c. 1850) by Peter F. Rothermel*

and exhibited at the John Brown House Museum in Providence. While the museum has many interesting exhibits and artifacts, none is quite as popular as this purportedly carnivorous root.

As with his lost grave site, history hasn't always treated Roger Williams gently. In 1877, Providence city workers accidentally blew up Slate Rock, the spot where Williams first arrived in Rhode Island.

URBAN SURF

Where do pasty Providence art students periodically emerge from their studios in search of sun?

Downtown Providence has plenty of waterfront but no beaches. Yet spend a little time in town and you'll hear people refer to "RISD Beach," and it's not a tall tale used to torment freshmen at the Rhode Island School of Design (RISD). RISD Beach is real, and in fact it's just one of two "beaches" that are the domain of sun-seeking students at the school.

Providence's RISD Beach lacks even an abstract artist's conception of an actual beach in that it has neither water nor sand. Rather, it's a triangular patch of lawn on RISD's College Hill campus between Waterman and Angell streets, presided over by *Daybreak*, a sculpture by Gilbert Franklin. On any sufficiently warm day you'll find students sprawled out on beach blankets, sunbathing, playing guitars, and basically doing things that you'd expect creative young people to do between classes.

RISD BEACH

WHAT: Sandless summer hangout for students

WHERE: Corner of Benefit, Angell, and Waterman sts., Providence

COST: Free

PRO TIP: The official name of RISD Beach is the Homer Lawn, which has been the site of countless student art exhibitions over the years— including the satirical one that originally launched the RISD Beach nickname.

Daybreak sculptor, RISD grad and art professor Gilbert Franklin also created *Orpheus Rising*, which can be seen on the school's Frazier Terrace.

RISD Beach on the Rhode Island School of Design campus in Providence (Rhode Island School of Design)

RISD students have access to a real beach, too. Tillinghast Place on Nayatt Road in Barrington serves as a satellite education, event, and recreation facility. Known locally as the RISD Farm, the 35-acre property includes a private beach, picnic tables, and gazebo, and is open to RISD students, faculty, and staff only. It, too, sometimes is referred to as "RISD Beach."

PRINCELY PUP

Why is there a statue of a domesticated dog in Providence's zoo?

One of the most popular animals in the Roger Williams Park Zoo isn't particularly exotic, or even alive, for that matter. Near the restaurant and gift shop at the heart of the zoo you'll find *The Sentinel*, a cast bronze statue of a dog with a broken chain, its back rubbed to a high gloss by the hands and bottoms of the countless children who have climbed aboard for photos over the years.

The statue is cute, and of course kids love dogs, but it's not immediately obvious why a zoo would include a statue of a common pet. But *The Sentinel* honors no ordinary dog.

Sculptor Thomas Frederick Hoppin was sleeping in his house in Providence one night in 1849 when he was awakened by the barking of his dog, Black Prince. The alert dog roused the entire Hoppin family—breaking his chain in the process—because the house was on fire. Thanks to this protective pup, everyone inside was able to escape the blaze safely.

In gratitude, Hoppin designed *The Sentinel*, which was cast in bronze by the Gorham Company and installed on the front lawn of what's now known as the Thomas F. Hoppin House at 383 Benefit Street. The tribute to this lifesaving pup remained

ROGER WILLIAMS PARK ZOO

WHAT: The Sentinel dog statue

WHERE: Roger Williams Park Zoo, 1000 Elmwood Ave., Providence

COST: Zoo admission is $19.95 for adults, $13.95 for kids

PRO TIP: In addition to a myriad of zoo animals, Roger Williams Park is home to the Providence Police Department's Mounted Command, including stables for the unit's Clydesdale, Percheron, and draft horses.

The Sentinel *(Roger Williams Park Zoo)*

at the landmark Italianate palazzo-style home for many years before being moved to the zoo.

The Sentinel's fame extended far beyond Rhode Island's shores: the statue was exhibited at the Crystal Palace in London and was awarded a gold medal by the New York Academy of Design.

AN ELEPHANT NEVER FORGETS

Why did someone fire a bullet into the skull of Betty the Fabulous Learned Elephant?

Thanks to circuses, zoos, and nature parks, most modern Americans have seen an elephant in person at least once in their lives. That wasn't the case, however, in the 19th century, when elephants were the stuff of myths and legends, and seeing one live provoked a mix of wonder, terror, and superstition.

The latter proved to be the fatal undoing of Betty the Fabulous Learned Elephant, one of the first pachyderms put on public display in the United States.

Hakaliah Bailey, a patriarch of the Barnum & Bailey circus family, purchased the first Indian elephant brought to America, Big Bett, and toured her across the country before she was shot by a religious fanatic in 1816. Undeterred, Bailey acquired a second elephant, Little Bett, which became known as Betty the Fabulous Learned Elephant, and began to tour with her, even making stops in small towns like Chepachet.

It was on Betty's second visit to Chepachet that tragedy struck again. On May 25, 1826, shots rang out as Betty was being led across a bridge in the center of town. Several men stationed in the window of a grist mill fired at the elephant— possibly because of a belief that elephants were impervious to bullets, or perhaps for no better reason than for the thrill of killing such a large animal. A number of shots hit Betty in the head, killing her.

The most famous circus elephant of all, Jumbo, also came to a tragic end, hit and killed by a train in Canada in 1885.

MAY 25, 1826 — MAY 25, 1976
DIVERSE HANDS FIRED UPON
BETTY
ONE OF AMERICA'S FIRST ELEPHANTS
AT THE NORTH END OF THE
RUSTIC SPAN THAT ARCHED
CHEPACHET RIVER

GIVEN IN OBSERVATION OF THE
150TH ANNIVERSARY OF THE EVENT BY
RICHMOND AND EDNA KENT

Betty the Elephant plaque in Chepachet

No immediate consequences were suffered by the killers, although it's said that rough justice eventually found them. On the 150th anniversary of Betty's death, Rhode Island declared May 25 "Elephant Day" in Chepachet, and local residents installed a memorial plaque on the bridge spanning the Chepachet River acknowledging that "diverse hands" had a role in her killing.

BETTY THE ELEPHANT MEMORIAL

WHAT: Memorial to a slain elephant

WHERE: Chepachet River Bridge, Putnam Pike, Glocester

COST: Free

PRO TIP: The Brown & Hopkins Country Store at 1179 Putnam Pike was one of several Chepachet buildings that were around when Betty was assassinated; it's one of America's oldest stores, in continuous operation since 1809.

BUSY BEE

Why is there a giant honeybee holding a machine gun and a wrench at Quonset Point?

Quonset Point in North Kingstown once was one of the largest naval bases in the US, famed for developing the Quonset hut—the arch-roofed, steel buildings used as barracks, offices, and supply sheds by the military all over the world.

Less well-known, however, is that during World War II Quonset was home to the Davisville Naval Construction Battalion (CB) Center and the original home of the Seabees, the sailors-turned-construction-workers who helped build bases, lay down airfields, and repair facilities after attacks, often driving their tractors and other heavy equipment while under enemy fire.

In 1942, at the height of the war, Rhode Island resident Frank Iafrate, an amateur artist, was stationed at Quonset when an officer asked him to design a Disney-esque mascot for the CBs. Iafrate first considered a beaver, but quickly settled on an "industrious" bee, dubbing it the "Seabee" after the unit's initials.

The design included a winged bee wearing a Navy cap and holding a machine gun in two of its legs and a hammer, wrench, and other tools in the others. The Seabee quickly was adopted as the official mascot and symbol of the Seabees, and in 1970 Iafrate pitched in to paint a giant steel Fighting Seabee statue constructed by Seabees stationed at Quonset. After decades

SEABEE MUSEUM

WHAT: Seabee statue

WHERE: 21 Iafrate Way, North Kingstown

COST: Free

PRO TIP: Be sure to visit the adjacent Seabee Museum—housed in a Quonset hut, of course.

Seabee statue in Quonset Point

of guarding the gate to the base, the statue was moved to the Seabee Museum and Memorial Park, where it still stands today, appropriately, on Iafrate Way.

Walt Disney also designed a Seabee logo in 1943—a honeybee wearing a sailor hat with a blade of grass in its mouth and carrying a wrench and hammer.

ELUSIVE HEADSTONES

When can you visit the second-oldest Jewish burial ground in the US?

Newport's Touro Synagogue is the oldest Jewish house of worship in America, built in 1763 and a popular tourist attraction open for tours and with an informative museum. Far older, and less accessible, is the nearby Touro Cemetery, dedicated in 1677 and opening its imposing gates to the public just one day each year.

Every third Sunday in August, for just a few hours, visitors can wander among the ancient headstones inscribed in English, Hebrew, Spanish, Latin, and the Judeo-Spanish language Ladino—a testament to the far-reaching nature of the Jewish diaspora in the colonial era.

Egyptian columns guard the cemetery entrance, with carved downturned torches symbolizing the snuffing of the flame of life. The graves include that of Judah Touro, a Jewish philanthropist who helped fund both the cemetery and the synagogue; and Moses Seixas, who wrote a letter from the Jewish congregation of Newport to newly elected President George Washington, prompting a reply assuring that the new government of the United States would respect freedom of religion and worship for all.

Poet Henry Wadsworth Longfellow, who visited Newport in 1852, had to cajole his way into a visit and found the cemetery

---

Another secret aspect of Touro Synagogue is the hidden trapdoor under the bimah, the platform used for Torah readings, an escape route adopted by Jews persecuted during the Inquisition.

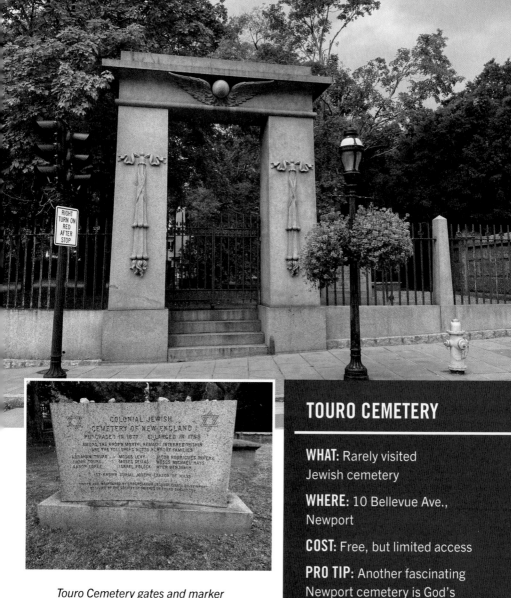

Touro Cemetery gates and marker

TOURO CEMETERY

WHAT: Rarely visited Jewish cemetery

WHERE: 10 Bellevue Ave., Newport

COST: Free, but limited access

PRO TIP: Another fascinating Newport cemetery is God's Little Acre on Farewell St., the most intact African American colonial-era burial ground in America.

inspiring, writing, "How strange it seems! These Hebrews in their graves, Close by the street of this fair seaport town, Silent beside the never-silent waves, At rest in all this moving up and down!" Almost 170 years later, it's still one of the most peaceful spots in Newport.

WHITE (PASTA) RIOT

Why did Italian immigrants once clash with police over macaroni?

Pasta long has been a staple in Italian food, so Italian immigrants on Providence's Federal Hill were getting a good case of agita in 1914 when—already battered by a slumping economy—they saw the cost of macaroni skyrocketing at local stores.

Local merchant F. P. Ventrone, who had a big store on the main street of Federal Hill, Atwells Avenue, already was in hot water with the local immigrant population after being accused of trying to pass off inferior American-made pasta as an import from the old country. Now, with rising prices stretching food budgets to the breaking point, Ventrone's store at 240–244 Atwells Avenue became a flashpoint for protests organized by the Italian Socialist Club.

A crowd of 2,000 people turned out on August 22, 1914, at the corner of Atwells Avenue and Dean Street to hear firebrand speakers denounce the rising prices on staples as well as the Providence police, who were thought to unfairly target the Italian community. The crowd that night dispersed quietly, but tensions still simmered.

On August 29 another rally was called, and this time tempers boiled over. The crowd moved down Atwells Avenue, smashing the windows on Ventrone's store. Police confronting the protesters opened fire on the crowd, and came under fire

ATWELLS AVENUE

WHAT: Providence macaroni riot site

WHERE: 240–244 Atwells Ave., Providence

COST: Free

PRO TIP: No marker or monument to the riots exists, but you can commemorate the event by noodling around Federal Hill and picking up some fresh pasta at the Venda Ravioli store in Providence's still-thriving Little Italy.

Historical photo of the Ventrone business block on Atwells Avenue
(Providence Warwick Convention and Visitors Bureau)

themselves. The next day brought another confrontation between protesters and police, and more gunfire. Eleven citizens, six police officers, and a fireman were injured in the melee. Similar skirmishes followed over the next few days before calm was restored and the Providence macaroni riots ended.

KICKED CAN

Who left a giant milk jug on the side of a road in Smithfield?

There was a time in America where the height of roadside marketing savvy was to build your store or restaurant inside a giant replica of the goods for sale inside—a snack bar housed in an oversized hamburger building, for example, or a music store in a tall, round building resembling a pile of long-playing (LP) records.

The Milk Can on State Route 146 in North Smithfield is one such roadside attraction. Built as an ice cream shop in 1929, the 31-foot, milk-jug-shaped building dished out cones and cups of frozen delights (and later, fast food) for decades before closing in 1968. The building has been vacant ever since; surprisingly, nobody has found a new use for the building in the last half century, although perhaps it's a bigger shock that vandals haven't burned it down by now.

At one point, the Milk Can was moved down the road about a mile by a new owner who hoped to renovate it, but the new site had hopelessly contaminated groundwater, and so the building still stands empty. One recent proposal was to redevelop the property and turn the Milk Can into a brewery—one that will no doubt prominently feature a milk stout on the menu.

MILK CAN BUILDING

WHAT: Former dairy bar in the shape of an old-style milk can

WHERE: Rte. 146 just north of Sayles Hill Rd., North Smithfield

COST: Free

PRO TIP: Just down the road from the Milk Can is a far more robust roadside relic: the Rustic Tri-View Drive-In, Rhode Island's only surviving drive-in movie theater, which has been in business since 1951.

Smithfield Milk Can

SUPERFICIAL READING

What kind of creepy library keeps books bound in human skin?

You've probably occasionally skimmed a book, but you probably haven't skinned one. Believe it or not, however, there was a time where it wasn't unheard of to bind a book in human skin. In fact, there's even a name for binding books in human leather: anthropodermic bibliopegy.

While the very idea seems sinister—and bookbinders did sometimes source their materials from the bodies of executed criminals—the four skin-bound books at Brown University's John Hay Library aren't volumes about the occult or serial murders, but rather cover anatomy, two collections of stories about death . . . and a novel about a man married to a lesbian.

The oldest of the books dates to 1568; the other grisly volumes were published in the 19th century. As you might imagine, you can't just go to the library's circulation desk and check these books out. Access is limited to researchers in order to protect the fragile bindings "and to minimize handling out of respect for the fact that they are [gulp] human remains." However, the library on Providence's Prospect Street does frequently showcase other parts of its fascinating collection of books and scholarly materials,

JOHN HAY LIBRARY

WHAT: Books bound in human skin

WHERE: John Hay Library, 20 Prospect St., Providence

COST: Free; some hours are restricted to Brown students and faculty only

PRO TIP: Speaking of creepy, Brown's Annmary Brown Memorial (21 Brown St.) is not only a library and art gallery, but also a mausoleum with a crypt containing the remains of Brown and her husband, General Rush Hawkins.

Brown University's John Hay Library

including permanent exhibits featuring a collection of historic swords, miniature soldiers, and paintings by Annmary Brown.

At least 18 anthropodermic books reside in libraries around the world, including the Boston Athenaeum's copy of highwayman James Allen's confession to the warden of the Massachusetts State Prison, which Allen requested to be bound in his own skin upon his death.

DREAD HEAD

Why is there a sultan staring down on the streets of Providence?

The Turk's Head building is one of the architectural gems of downtown Providence, an elegantly curved edifice in the same style as New York's Flatiron Building. The 16-story, 215-foot-tall building opened in 1916, and has always housed corporate offices, so there's nothing particularly fascinating inside. What gives the building its distinctive name is the ornately carved head and partial torso of an Ottoman warrior over the arched lobby entrance.

With a turban emblazoned with a crescent moon, long mustache, and piercing gaze, the carving seems anything but welcoming. The story of the Turk's Head far precedes the building it is mounted on. Before the office tower was raised, the corner of Weybosset Street and Westminster Street was occupied by a shop belonging to Jacob Whitman, dating back to 1750. At that time, when literacy was not as widespread, it was common for stores to use symbols in place of (or in addition to) lettered signs to advertise.

Back when Providence was a seafaring town, Whitman acquired a wooden figurehead from the sailing ship *Sultan* and mounted it on the front of his store. The shop literally was called

THE TURK'S HEAD BUILDING

WHAT: Menacing sculpture

WHERE: 76 Westminster St., Providence

COST: Free

PRO TIP: Cargo ships once sailed up the Providence River as far as Westminster St., docking in the river and the former Ship Street Canal. Remnants of Providence's mercantile past include the brick warehouses that still line the east side of the river.

The Turk's Head Building in Providence

"At the Sign of the Turk's Head," and became a local landmark for anyone navigating downtown Providence.

Whitman's house is long gone, but the architects of the office tower that replaced it were sure to replicate the ornamental warrior, this time in stone, and to this day the Turk's Head building is a familiar guidepost for Providence residents and visitors.

GAG ORDER

Why are Rhode Island's unique little hot dogs named after New York?

Besides stuffed quahogs and Del's Lemonade, there are few foods as authentically Rhode Island as the hot wiener. Yet the leading purveyor of these pint-sized hot dogs is called New York System Wieners. How does that even make sense?

The answer takes us all the way back to Coney Island in the early 1900s, when hot dogs were a novelty food and deeply connected in the public mind to New York. So the New York System Wieners and Coney Island System Wieners that opened in Providence in the 1910s and 1920s were simply looking to cash in on the association.

A Rhode Island wiener, however, is really nothing like a Nathan's Coney Island hot dog. Typically ordered in multiples, the diminutive wieners in their sweet buns are lined up on the grill man's forearm and slathered with a Greek-inspired meat sauce, diced onions, celery salt, and mustard.

Sometimes dubbed "gaggers," Rhode Island hot wieners are a late-night (often: after drinking) staple. You still can order them by the dozen at the Olneyville New York System Wieners restaurant, in business since 1941, as well as at other wiener shops like the Olneyville sister store in Cranston, Wien-O-Rama (also in Cranston), Ferucci's in West Warwick, E. P. Wieners in East Providence, Sam's in Warwick, and an armful of others.

NEW YORK SYSTEM WIENERS

WHAT: Tiny hot dogs

WHERE: Olneyville New York System Wieners, 18 Plainfield St., Providence

COST: $2.79 per wiener

PRO TIP: If you really want to look like a Rhode Islander, order coffee milk (made with local Autocrat Coffee Syrup) to wash down your wieners.

New York System wieners and coffee milk (Paul Kandarian)

MAGNETIC MYSTERY ROCKS

Where's the only place in the world you can find Cumberlandite?

Rhode Island has an official state rock, which in itself is odd enough. But it does make sense that Cumberlandite is that special stone, because it's a rock that can only be found in Rhode Island.

And not just in Rhode Island, but in one really small corner of the smallest state. Nearly all Cumberlandite originates from a single, four-acre quarry in the town of Cumberland.

The stone is very dense, has a high iron content (it's also rich in titanium) and appears brown or gray with white flecks. A type of igneous rock, Cumberlandite was formed about 1.5 billion years ago when molten lava mixed with a variety of minerals (relax: Rhode Island doesn't have any volcanoes now).

Honestly, Cumberlandite is not the most attractive of rocks. But early settlers used it to make farm tools, and even tried (unsuccessfully) to build cannons from it. Some scammers tried to pass the rocks off as meteorites. But maybe the most lasting legacy for Cumberlandite can be found in the Ballou Cemetery in

BLACKALL/BALLOU PRESERVE

WHAT: Rhode Island's magnetic state rock

WHERE: Blackall/Ballou Preserve, 8 Old W Wrentham Rd., Cumberland

COST: Free

PRO TIP: Although Cumberlandite is unique to Cumberland, glacier-deposited pieces of the rock also can be found in a few other places in the state, including Blackstone Park and the Swan Point Cemetery along the Seekonk River in Providence.

Cumberlandite in nature and on display (Dave Brown)

Cumberland, where a number of headstones were carved from Cumberlandite.

An old Cumberlandite quarry is located in the woods behind the cemetery, and the rocks also may be found while exploring the trails of the Cumberland Land Trust's nearby Blackall/Ballou Preserve; bring a magnet if you want to pick up a piece of this unique Rhode Island rock.

HUNG, DRAWN, AND QUARTERED

Why did the Puritans single out a Rhode Island man for a horrific execution?

Being hung, drawn, and quartered is a sanitized description for hanging a prisoner, then cutting him down before he strangles, disemboweling him while still alive, then cutting off his limbs and genitals.

Reserved for the crime of treason under English law, this punishment was administered in America only once, at Smith's Castle in North Kingstown. In 1676, Joshua Tefft of what was then known as Kingstown was accused of aiding the Narragansett tribe in a battle against a Puritan army that had invaded Rhode Island during King Philip's War. Tefft, who was friendly with his Native American neighbors, allegedly fired on the Puritans as they launched an unprovoked attack on the Narragansetts in what became known as the Great Swamp Massacre.

Captured and convicted of treason by a Puritan court, Tefft was hung, drawn, and quartered on January 18, 1676, at Smith's Castle in Wickford, also known as Cocumscussoc. The Narragansetts later burned the fortified house, but William Smith

SMITH'S CASTLE

WHAT: Site of a gruesome colonial-era execution

WHERE: Smith's Castle, 55 Richard Smith Dr., North Kingstown

COST: Grounds are free; house tours are $10 for adults, $5 for children

PRO TIP: For a unique view of Smith's Castle, launch a kayak from Wilson Park into Mill Cove, where you can see the sedate homestead from the water and paddle around Rabbit Island, given by the Narragansett tribe to Roger Williams to graze his goats.

Smith's Castle and stocks

rebuilt his home in 1678, and it still stands today. The grounds of Smith's Castle, now a museum, include the burial site of 40 English men killed in King Philip's War, but not a grave for Tefft, whose head was stuck on a fence post at the fort and later was disposed of in an unknown location.

A WHALE OF A SAD TALE

Where can you see the remains of a lighthouse destroyed by a hurricane?

The Whale Rock lighthouse had a fishy reputation during its 50-odd years of service. Built in 1882 to protect mariners in the West Passage of Narragansett Bay, Whale Rock was the scene of a violent knife and shotgun battle between two lighthouse keepers in 1897, and even when keepers weren't battling to the death it was a damp and lonely place to work.

Plus, lighthouse keepers complained that the Whale Rock light wasn't well-built, and that proved tragically true on the night of September 21, 1938, when the Great New England Hurricane roared into Narragansett Bay. The winds of the powerful storm pushed a 15-foot storm surge against the exposed lighthouse. After several hours of battering, the wind and waves ripped the lighthouse from its foundation, killing lighthouse keeper Walter Eberle, whose body was never found.

The broken lighthouse sits at the bottom of Narragansett Bay, but its foundation still is visible to boaters: a lighted beacon now warns them away from the still-

WHALE ROCK LIGHTHOUSE

WHAT: Lighthouse knocked down by a hurricane

WHERE: Whale Rock Trail, 33 Harvey Ln., Narragansett

COST: Free

PRO TIP: The tragedy of the 1938 hurricane was widespread: 262 people died in the storm, including seven children whose school bus was washed away at Mackerel Cove on Jamestown.

The metal remains of the lighthouse are still scattered across the sea floor all around Whale Rock.

The remnants of the Whale Rock Lighthouse

dangerous Whale Rock. The remains of the lighthouse also can be seen from the Whale Rock Trail, a hiking path in Narragansett. The short, out-and-back trail runs from Boston Neck Road through grasslands and onto the rocky shoreline and to a small beach. From the rocks you have a clear view of Whale Rock and the base of the lighthouse.

NINE MEN'S MISERY

Where can you find the oldest military memorial in the United States?

King Philip's War, which pitted European colonists against the Native American inhabitants of New England, was a brutal affair. Waged between 1675 and 1678, the war included massacres of women and children, the burning of cities, murder, enslavement, and torture.

One of the more vicious episodes in the war took place in 1676, when a force of 60 English troops from Massachusetts and 20 Wampanoag allies were ambushed by Narragansett fighters. All but 10 of the invaders were killed, and the Narragansetts tortured the survivors. All but one died.

The mutilated bodies of the victims soon were discovered and buried at the site, with a stone cairn placed over their remains. And for nearly 350 years a memorial has been maintained at what became known as Nine Men's Misery; the current marker was placed by the state of Rhode Island in 1928 and was maintained by an order of Trappist monks who purchased the property as a monastery.

CUMBERLAND MONASTERY

WHAT: First military monument in America

WHERE: Cumberland Monastery, 1464 Diamond Hill Rd., Cumberland

COST: Free

PRO TIP: Some parts of the old Monastery of Our Lady of the Valley complex remain in use in the Cumberland Public Library. The cloisters, built with granite quarried on-site by the Trappist monks, now is the library's second floor, while the former Chapter Room serves as the library's Community Room.

Nine Men's Misery memorial

After the monastery burned down in 1950, the town of Cumberland regained control of the memorial; it's located in the woods of what's still known as the Cumberland Monastery on Diamond Hill Road. Behind the public library that now occupies the site are more than a dozen hiking trails through the 481-acre property: the one you want is the Nine Men's Misery Trail.

REACH THE BEACHES

Where are Rhode Island's four "secret" beaches located?

It's not often that a state as old as Rhode Island gains new public access to the sea. When the military abandoned the former Naval Air Station Quonset Point in 1974, the base was handed over to the state for redevelopment. But it took until the 21st century to reclaim four stretches of the former base's Narragansett Bay coastline as public beaches.

Each of the often-overlooked Quonset beaches has its own unique charms. Calf Pasture Beach is located at the end of the Quonset Bike Path; it's the longest beach of the four, and perfect for visitors seeking a stretch of sand all to themselves. Blue Beach has dunes and a nice view of the village of Wickford and its harbor, while Spink's Neck Beach is a popular launch spot for sea kayaks and a great spot for watching giant auto carriers sailing in and out of the Port of Davisville. Compass Rose Beach, once a seaplane base, has the best waves and is near the end

QUONSET POINT

WHAT: Quonset's secret beaches

WHERE: Quonset Point, North Kingstown

COST: Free

PRO TIP: The off-road Quonset Bike Path runs for 3.7 miles from Post Road to Calf Pasture Point; Calf Pasture Beach is the one Quonset beach that doesn't have parking, so biking is the best way to get there.

Quonset is an Algonquian word meaning "small, long place"—a pretty decent description of Quonset's four secret beaches.

Boats on Compass Rose Beach

of the runway of Quonset State Airport, so you're likely to see a lot of low-level civilian and military planes flying overhead.

Located in the middle of an industrial park and an airfield, the Quonset beaches are unknown even to many Rhode Islanders. In terms of waves and atmosphere, they can't really compare to the beautiful ocean beaches of South County, but they're uncrowded, most have plenty of parking, and they're free and open to everyone.

SWAMP SPAN

Where is Rhode Island's only true covered bridge?

Can a state really be in New England and not have a covered bridge? Historically, Rhode Island had several, including the India Point Covered Bridge, the first covered interstate railroad bridge in the United States. By 1920, however, all of the state's covered bridges had been replaced by more functional but less photogenic concrete spans.

Rhode Island remained bereft of covered bridges until 1993, when a traditional truss-construction covered bridge was raised over Hemlock Brook on Central Pike in Foster to commemorate the 350th anniversary of Rhode Island's founding. That bridge lasted less than four months before it was set ablaze by vandals, but the town of Foster quickly rebuilt and rededicated the 36-foot-long Swamp Meadow Covered Bridge in 1994.

The bridge is a replica of the 19th-century covered bridge that once stood at the same spot. Central Pike is a pretty detour running through the woods parallel to busy US Route 6, a nice country drive that includes a passage over the Barden Reservoir as well as the covered bridge.

Rhode Island actually has a longer covered bridge—a 55-footer—at the entrance of Lincoln Woods State Park in Lincoln. The bridge, which spans the Moshassuck River, also

SWAMP MEADOW COVERED BRIDGE

WHAT: Rhode Island's only covered bridge

WHERE: 105A Central Pike, Foster

COST: Free

PRO TIP: Raise a toast to Rhode Island's only covered bridge at the nearby Nickel Creek Vineyard at 12 King Rd.; the winery offers wine tastings and seating in its rustic vineyards.

The Swamp Meadow Covered Bridge

is beautiful, but it's not considered a true covered bridge because it lacks truss construction—how's that for a little bridge nerd trivia for you?

Wooden bridges in New England were typically covered to protect them from weather, increasing their average life span from 20 years for an uncovered bridge to 100 years for a covered one.

WATERY GRAVES

What are the drowned villages of Rhode Island?

Kent, Richmond, South Scituate, Ashland, Saundersville, Rockland, Ponaganset. Look at a map of Rhode Island prior to the 1920s and you'll find these small villages dotting the town of Scituate in northern Rhode Island. Look now, and you'll see nothing but water.

These towns all were drowned when the Scituate Reservoir was built to provide drinking water for the city of Providence, along with parts of North Scituate and Clayville. More than 1,000 buildings were destroyed or moved in the process; the reservoir even obliterated an entire railroad.

Completed in 1926, the 5.3-square-mile reservoir filled long stretches of the North Branch Pawtuxet River, the Moswansicut River, and the Ponaganset River. Between the land taken for the reservoir and surrounding land acquired as a buffer to protect the water supply, hundreds of Rhode Islanders were displaced by the project; some committed suicide, so distraught they were about being forced from their homes.

The reservoir contains 28 islands that almost nobody ever visits because public access is prohibited, but even on these high points of land any existing buildings were removed. Yet a few ghostly reminders of the drowned villages remain. The Gainer Dam that holds back the reservoir's 37 billion gallons of water is close to the former village of Kent. Bodies from local cemeteries were dug up and reburied in the New Rockland Cemetery on

SCITUATE RESERVOIR

WHAT: Vanished villages in Northern Rhode Island

WHERE: Underneath the Scituate Reservoir

COST: Free

PRO TIP: The best view of the reservoir is from the Scituate Reservoir Bridge on State Rte. 14/Plainfield Pike.

Top: The Scituate Reservoir

Inset: Rockland Car Barn
(Providence Public Library)

Plainfield Pike. The woods around the reservoir are full of old stone walls, a reminder of the farmers' fields that once filled the area. And if you look at Google Maps you can still see the faint outlines of a road where the Central Pike (also called Central Avenue) was cleaved in two by the reservoir.

The Scituate Reservoir is the largest lake in Rhode Island and is filled with about 39 billion gallons of fresh water.

WAT'S UP, BUDDHA?

Why is there a miniature version of Cambodia's Angkor Wat temple in Cranston?

It's unusual enough to see a giant Buddha statue in suburban Cranston, but the smiling, 10-foot, robed founder of Buddhism is only part of the story at the Wat Dhamagosnaram Buddhist Temple on Plainfield Pike. Spread out at the Buddha's feet is a 260-square-foot replica of the majestic Angkor Wat temple in Cambodia, one of the world's great centers of Buddhism.

Hand-carved in Cambodia, the miniature recreation of the 12th-century Angkor Wat complex features buildings, gates, statuary, and of course the famous spired main temple building. While the real Angkor Wat occupies about 500 acres, making it the largest religious structure in the world, the Cranston version is confined to the front lawn of the Buddhist temple.

Just as Angkor Wat is a pilgrimage site for Buddhists from around the world, the monks who tend the Cranston temple welcome visitors to view the Angkor Wat model and tour the temple grounds, which include statues of other Buddhist deities as well as the Dalai Lama. To see an even bigger Buddha, visit the Rhode Island School of Design Museum in Providence, which has a 14-foot carved

WAT DHAMAGOSNARAM BUDDHIST TEMPLE

WHAT: Buddhist temple with Angkor Wat model

WHERE: 2870 Plainfield Pike, Cranston

COST: Free

PRO TIP: If you want to immerse yourself in Buddhism, the Providence Zen Center in Cumberland has a 62-foot-tall Peace Pagoda and offers daily public meditation sessions, as well as residential stays and retreats.

Angkor Wat temple model

wooden statue of the deity called the Buddha Mahāvairocana on display. This big Buddha, like Angkor Wat, dates from around the 12th century, but comes from Japan, not Cambodia.

The Providence metropolitan area has among the top 10 biggest Cambodian populations in the US, with about 8,000 residents of Cambodian descent.

FUNKY FLEUR

How did a Norman-style home end up on one of Providence's most prominent colonial streets?

Thomas Street in Providence is part of the East Side's treasure house of colonial architecture. The current clubhouse of the Providence Art Club was built in 1790 and may have been the first brick home in Providence. The Deacon Edward Taylor House is older still, built in 1784. Both face the First Baptist Church in America, completed in 1775.

And then there's the house at 7 Thomas Street.

Known as the Fleur de Lys Studio, it was constructed in the half-timbered style that had its heyday in 16th-century Europe. Painted in an eye-catching (or garish, depending on your perspective) mustard yellow on the bottom floor, the building is adorned with stuccoed artwork and features painted panels depicting sculpture, painting, and architecture on the second-floor facade.

The building doesn't date to the Renaissance period, however: it was designed in 1886 by artist Sydney Burleigh and architect Edmund Wilson. A landmark building in the Arts and Crafts Movement, the house was home to Burleigh's Fleur de Lys Studio and remains a center for the visual arts, still housing artist studios. It's now owned by the Providence Art Club, which opens its doors to the public for studio tours and artist exhibitions.

FLEUR DE LYS STUDIO

WHAT: Unique half-timbered building in Providence

WHERE: 7 Thomas St., Providence

COST: Free

PRO TIP: The Providence Art Club's three galleries are open to the public Sunday to Friday from 12 to 4 p.m.

Fleur de Lys building

GIVING PROPS

How did a pair of German U-boat screws end up on display at the Naval War College in Newport?

One of the last battles of World War II took place off the coast of Rhode Island. On May 5, 1945, the same day that Germany surrendered to the Allies, the German submarine *U-853* torpedoed the collier SS *Black Point* off of Point Judith, blowing off the ship's stern and sending her to the bottom. Four American warships then tracked down the submarine seven miles east of Block Island, sinking it the next day.

A single body of an unidentified German sailor was recovered from the wreckage of the sub in 1960, and was buried with full military honors in the Island Cemetery Annex on Van Zandt Avenue. Despite the submarine's status as a wartime grave, however, it was looted repeatedly over the years. Somehow, the twin brass propellers from *U-853* wound up on the lawn of the Inn at Castle Hill, a local hotel, where they remained for decades before being acquired by the Naval War College, located on Coasters Island in Newport.

The propellers were formally donated by the German government to the US Navy, which in turn built a memorial to the sailors lost in the Battle of Point Judith with the twin props as the centerpiece. Visitors can easily visit the unknown

U-853 MEMORIAL

WHAT: Propellers from German U-boat sunk off Block Island in 1945

WHERE: Naval War College, 686 Cushing Rd., Newport

COST: Free

PRO TIP: The Naval War College, including the *U-583* memorial and the Naval War College Museum, is a secure military facility, so contact the base for preapproval before visiting.

Top: U-853 *and crew*

Inset: U-853 *memorial at the Naval War College (Cmdr. Gary Ross, USN)*

sailor grave in the Island Cemetery; public access to the Naval War College has been limited since 9/11, which makes seeing the *U-853* memorial a bit of a challenge. Scuba divers also can view the wreck of the submarine, but the *U-853* lies in 130 feet of water, so that's for experienced deep-sea divers only.

STARS IN THE BUCKET

Whoever thought Pawtucket, aka "The Bucket," could become "Hollywood East"?

Little Rhode Island has some decent star power when it comes to Hollywood moviemaking: Academy Award winner Viola Davis grew up in Central Falls and graduated from Rhode Island College, and some of the top comedic filmmakers of the last few decades, including the Farrelly brothers (*Dumb and Dumber*, *There's Something about Mary*) and *Family Guy* creator Seth MacFarlane (a Rhode Island School of Design grad), have Rhody roots.

But there's no more of a Rhode Island homeboy in the directorial ranks than Michael Corrente, the Pawtucket-born filmmaker responsible for *Outside Providence*, *Federal Hill*, and *American Buffalo*. It was during the making of the latter in 1996 that Corrente returned to his hometown with Hollywood A-lister Dustin Hoffman, Dennis Franz

PAWTUCKET HOLLYWOOD WALK OF FAME

WHAT: Movie star handprints

WHERE: 3 Exchange St., Pawtucket

COST: Free

PRO TIP: Seth MacFarlane has a star on the Hollywood Walk of Fame, but Woody Allen doesn't, so Pawtucket is as good as it gets for street monuments to the famously bespectacled director.

More than 50 movies have been filmed in Rhode Island, from *Dumb and Dumber* to *Moonrise Kingdom*. More recently, *Hocus Pocus 2* was filmed in various locations in the state, including Chase Farm in Lincoln.

Woody Allen handprints in the streets of Pawtucket

(best known for his work on *NYPD Blue*), and Sean Nelson to film the adaptation of a David Mamet play.

During filming, Corrente convinced his three stars to join him in putting their handprints and signatures into wet cement in Pawtucket's Times Square; a few years later, director Woody Allen, in town to film *Irrational Man* with Emma Stone and Joaquin Phoenix, added his imprint, as well.

That's pretty much all the action that the "Hollywood Walk of Fame East" has generated, however, and the site in front of the historic Beswick Building has gotten pretty beaten-up over the years. Someone has made off with the gold stars, but you can still see the handprints and signatures on the well-trodden sidewalk.

CEMETERY CARVERS

**Where have Newporters been going since 1704
to be immortalized in stone?**

If you died in Newport during the American Revolution, chances are your headstone would have been carved at the John Stevens Shop on Thames Street. And the same might be true if fate happened to put its crooked finger on you in the 21st century.

Located at 29 Thames Street, the John Stevens stonecutting shop opened in 1704 and has carved memorials without interruption for more than 300 years, making it one of the longest-operating businesses in America. The Stevens family ran the shop for over two centuries, and it is currently owned by the third generation of the Benson family, which bought the business in 1927.

Newport's Common Burying Ground is filled with 17th- and 18th-century headstones carved at the Stevens Shop, and the Bensons not only designed headstones for the likes of Tennessee Williams and George Balanchine, but also engraved the Iwo Jima and John F. Kennedy memorials in Arlington National Cemetery. The company has done work on the National World War II Memorial, the Martin Luther King Jr. Memorial in Washington, DC, and many others, too.

JOHN STEVENS SHOP

WHAT: Semi-immortal headstone artisans

WHERE: John Stevens Shop, 29 Thames St., Newport

COST: Free

PRO TIP: Stevens-carved headstones can be found in Newport's Common Burying Ground, such as at the 1769 grave of Capt. Nathaniel Waldron.

Top: John
Stevens Shop

Inset: Newport
headstones

Closer to home, visitors can see the company's work on the stone markers in Newport's Trinity Square. You can also drop by the shop on Thames Street for a walk back through time—you'll know it by its colonial architecture and dark green façade, although curiously there's no marker indicating its presence.

NAZI PUP

How did the collar of Hitler's favorite dog end up in a former department store in Wakefield?

Anyone who thinks a dog is a good judge of character obviously never heard about Adolf Hitler's dog, Blondi. The German Shepherd may have been the dictator's oldest and best friend—in fact, Blondi was probably Hitler's only real friend. In the end, though, it didn't matter.

Given to the Nazi dictator as a puppy by his private secretary, Martin Bormann, in 1941, the dog stayed with Hitler throughout the Second World War. Blondi went into the bunker in Berlin with Hitler where the Nazi dictator spent his final days. As Soviet troops closed in, Hitler ordered his doctors to test his cyanide suicide pills on Blondi.

The dog was buried close to the hole where Hitler's body was dumped after he killed himself, but somehow Blondi's swastika-embossed collar ended up surviving, likely snatched up as a war souvenir. Acquired by a collector for the International Museum of World War II in Natick, Massachusetts, it was later donated to the International Museum of World War II in South Kingstown, which currently has the collar on display at its museum in the former Kenyon's Department Store in Wakefield.

Blondi's collar is just one of the many fascinating artifacts at the museum, whose other exhibits include a hull section from

INTERNATIONAL MUSEUM OF WORLD WAR II

WHAT: Collar of Hitler's dog, Blondi

WHERE: International Museum of World War II, 344 Main St., South Kingstown

COST: $10 for adults, children free

PRO TIP: Every museum visitor gets to walk away with one of the foundation's World War II documentary films.

Top: Hitler and Eva Braun with their dogs; Blondi is on the right (Bundesarchiv).

Inset: Blondi's dog collar (National World War 2 Foundation)

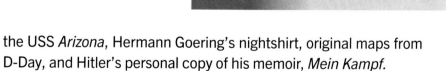

the USS *Arizona*, Hermann Goering's nightshirt, original maps from D-Day, and Hitler's personal copy of his memoir, *Mein Kampf*.

Hitler was said to love Blondi more than his mistress, Eva Braun, yet would beat the dog as punishment for disobedience.

CREAMY CABINETS

Who knew that a drink named after furniture could be so good?

Unless you're a termite or a beaver, you've likely never considered consuming a cabinet. But in Rhode Island, you'll find them delicious.

In local parlance a "cabinet" is another word for a milkshake or a frappe, and the pinnacle of the art is the Coffee Cabinet, made with coffee syrup (another Rhode Island beverage favorite), vanilla ice cream, and milk.

Dating from the early 20th century and likely introduced by the state's coffee-loving Italian population, the cabinet may get its nickname from the furniture in which blenders were stored.

If you have a blender, it's pretty easy to make a cabinet at home—just pick up some ice cream, milk, and coffee syrup from Autocrat or Dave's and you're good to go. But if you want to sip one in style, head to the Delekta Pharmacy on Main Street in Warren, a former drugstore that retains its vintage soda fountain and serves various flavors

Rhode Island actually has two famous milkshakes: the other is the Awful Awful, sold at the eight Newport Creamery restaurants scattered across the state.

A coffee cabinet (Paul Kandarian)

of cabinets, including vanilla, chocolate, creamsicle, and of course coffee blended with homemade syrup, following an old family recipe.

Coffee milk, by the way, is Rhode Island's state drink, and if you want to sample the state's coffee-flavored beverage without the ice cream, it's fairly common to find coffee milk on restaurant menus in the state, notably at old-school eateries like New York System Wieners.

PARTITIONED PRUDENCE

Why was Prudence Island cut in half?

The woods of Rhode Island are filled with ancient stone walls, but while most were raised to make the boundaries of farmers' fields, the Division Wall on Prudence Island is a reminder of one of the state's first land deals.

Roger Williams and John Winthrop, the two men most responsible for founding what would eventuality become the state of Rhode Island, purchased Prudence Island from the Narragansett tribe in 1637. Williams wanted the north end of the 5.5-square-mile island in Narragansett Bay, while Winthrop laid claim to the south end. So, they agreed to build a stone wall from one side of the island to the other to separate their property.

The so-called Division Wall runs for more than a mile from the east to west shores of Prudence Island; on the west end is Pulpit Rock, a large glacial boulder where Williams once preached to island inhabitants.

You can follow the wall pretty much from one side of Prudence Island to the other on the Division Wall Trail, part of an extensive network of hiking trails in the center of the island. Lightly populated and completely cut off from the mainland except for ferry service from Bristol, peaceful Prudence Island would still be recognizable to Williams and Winthrop: most of the island is protected parkland.

PRUDENCE ISLAND

WHAT: Prudence Island Division Wall

WHERE: Prudence Island (Division Wall Trail)

COST: Free

PRO TIP: Bring your bike over on the Prudence Island Ferry for a day of exploring Rhode Island's largest island accessible only by boat.

The Division Wall on Prudence Island

BLACK DIAMOND

Where can you hike up old ski trails in Rhode Island?

Given how flat Rhode Island is, visitors often are surprised to learn that the state is home to one operating ski area (Yawgoo Valley in Exeter) and also had several others that are now sadly defunct. One of the latter was Diamond Hill Ski Area in Cumberland, where local skiers carved and schussed from around 1935 until the early 1980s.

There once were two ski areas on Diamond Hill, an outcrop of mica-infused white quartz whose 481-foot summit is Everest-scale by Rhode Island standards. On the backside of the hill was Ski Valley, which operated from 1962 to 1985, when it was sold for redevelopment as a condominium complex. On the front side of the hill, closest to Diamond Hill Road, the state of Rhode Island operated the Diamond Hill ski area, which at its peak featured two chairlifts and multiple ski trails down the mountain.

When the ski areas shut down, the town of Cumberland converted the 373-acre property into Diamond Hill Town Park,

DIAMOND HILL TOWN PARK

WHAT: Former ski area turned public park

WHERE: Diamond Hill Town Park, 4125 Diamond Hill Rd., Cumberland

COST: Free

PRO TIP: The snow-covered ski trails at Diamond Hill may no longer be active, but you can still chill out with frozen treats at the Ice Cream Machine snack bar across the street.

Before it was a ski area, the current Diamond Hill Town Park was the site of granite and copper mines.

Top: Diamond Hill Ski
Area around 1970
(Postcard from collection
of Louis McGowan)

Inset: Diamond Hill today

which features a concert bandshell, a pond, and 3.8 miles of hiking
trails, many of which follow the old ski trails to the summit of the
"Big Hill."

Anyone familiar with the layout of a ski area will immediately
recognize the somewhat grown-in but still broad trails from the
location of the former base lodge—some look like they still would
be fun to ski during the next big snowfall. Other remnants of the old
ski operations include the bases of old lift towers and a water tank
marked "Ski Valley" at the summit, where on a clear day you can
see all the way to the Boston skyline.

PLUCKED CLUCK

Where can you get a live chicken in one of Rhode Island's most popular tourist spots?

Rhode Island has a thing for chickens: the Rhode Island Red is the state bird, and family-style dinners at Wright's Chicken Farm in Nasonville are a tradition that goes back several generations. But there's no greater old-school poultry purveyor in Providence than Antonelli's on Federal Hill.

ANTONELLI POULTRY

WHAT: Store selling live poultry on Federal Hill

WHERE: Antonelli Poultry, 62 De Pasquale Ave., Providence

COST: Free

PRO TIP: Look for the big chicken statue outside of Antonelli's on DePasquale Square, a place at the heart of Federal Hill filled with outdoor cafés.

Long before we all bought meat neatly wrapped in plastic wrap farmers would sell live or freshly slaughtered and cleaned chickens to go into the dinner pot. And that's still the way it's done at Antonelli Poultry, which has occupied a no-frills shop in a corner of DePasquale Square since the neighborhood was populated by Italian immigrants off the boat from Ellis Island. These days the customers still are mostly immigrants, but hail from Latin America instead. Backyard chicken farmers also sometimes bring their hens in to be slaughtered when their egg-laying days are done.

Walk inside Antonelli's and you'll be greeted by the squawking of the live birds kept out back. If you want to see your next meal face-to-face you can pick your own chicken, or just order one sight unseen and it will be cleaned and processed for you. In addition to fresh, live chickens, Antonelli sells Thanksgiving turkeys, ducks, rabbits, guinea hens, pheasant,

Antonelli Poultry (Rhode Island Commerce Corp.)

quail, goat, and partridge meat, as well as eggs from various fowl—
more things you're not likely to find at your local Stop & Shop.

Turkeys, chickens, ducks, and, more rarely,
quail still find a place on American plates,
but in the 19th century people consumed a
far wider variety of birds, including pigeons
and robins.

CLOISTERED COOKIES

Where can you find a "hermit" that you'd like to eat?

If you want an authentic taste of New England culinary history, head to Wright's Dairy Farm & Bakery in North Smithfield— one of the few places in Rhode Island where you can buy the elusive "hermit" cookies that have been a traveler's favorite for centuries.

WRIGHT'S DAIRY FARM

WHAT: Traditional New England cookies

WHERE: Wright's Dairy Farm & Bakery, 200 Woonsocket Hill Rd., North Smithfield

COST: Between $8 and $9 for a one-pound bag of hermits

PRO TIP: Visitors are welcome to watch the farm's dairy cows get milked each day at 3 p.m.

Made with flour, brown sugar or molasses, spices, and dried fruit, hermits are prized for their ability to resist spoilage without refrigeration for months; the fact that they often remained stored indefinitely in a dark cabinet before being eaten may have earned them their unusual name. Hermits were eaten in rural farmhouses before electricity, by sailors on long voyages, and by soldiers serving far from home.

The Wright's Farm hermit recipe calls for raisins, cloves,

Wright's also sells bakery pizza, another unusual local food consisting of a flat crust topped with tomato sauce and olive oil, but no cheese. It may sound like sacrilege to exclude cheese from pizza, but bakery pizza is a savory treat that you'll find at almost any backyard party in Rhode Island.

Hermit cookies

cinnamon, and ginger, and the cookies can be purchased at the bakeshop or ordered online. They taste best washed down with fresh milk from the Wright's dairy.

A WHOLE LOTTA LOTUS

How did an Asian lotus garden end up growing in North Kingstown?

Take a summer drive down State Route 1A in North Kingstown, and you might be startled by a sight more common in Asia than New England: a thriving lotus pond with enormous white and pink flowers in bloom, just off the shoulder of the road.

The Indian lotuses (*Nelumbo nucifera*), also known as the sacred lotus, are located in a waterway that once fed the nearby Hamilton Mill, a textile mill that operated for about 130 years before closing in 1978 and being converted into condominiums. The still, murky waters of the old control lagoon turned out to be an ideal environment for the tropical lotus plants—which can live for hundreds and even thousands of years—to thrive in the warm weather and survive the cold New England winters.

The Hamilton Mills condo conversion is what gave North Kingstown its lotuses. The developers wanted to spruce up the property, and landscapers recognized the potential of the lagoon as a lotus pond. Planted in 1982 and still growing strong almost 40 years later, the lotuses have become a popular tourist stop when the flowers are in midsummer bloom.

The leaves of the lotus plants can spread up to 31 inches wide, and the flowering stalks reach six feet into the water and mud below. The seeds of the lotus are edible, but visitors

North Kingstown lotus pond

are prohibited from touching or taking these hardy botanical immigrants to Rhode Island. You're welcome to stop and snap as many photos as you'd like, however.

ROBERT THE HERMIT

Who was the former slave who once lived under a Providence bridge?

If you had a life as tragic as that of Robert Voorhis, you'd probably avoid people, too. Born into slavery in New Jersey in 1770, Voorhis was separated from his family at age four when his master sent him to serve his daughter in Georgetown, which was part of Maryland at the time. As a young man, Voorhis fell in love with a woman who promised to marry him on the condition that he become a free man. A white friend promised to help Voorhis win his freedom, so he got married, and the couple had children together.

It was then, however, that the friend betrayed Voorhis, selling him to a South Carolina slave trader. Voorhis never saw his family again, and after several escape attempts managed to make his way to New England, endured hardships at sea as a sailor as well as a second, unhappy marriage.

Having failed to find his first love, Voorhis determined to cut himself off from society. He built what was described as a stone cave on a patch of land in East Providence (then a part of Seekonk, Massachusetts), mostly keeping to himself in a thick grove of pine trees. There, he lived for about 17 years with the consent of the owner of the land, who occasionally offered support.

Having heard tales of the Providence hermit, writer Henry Trumbull sought out Voorhis and persuaded him to tell his life story, which was published in pamphlet form in 1829. Despite

EAST PROVIDENCE

WHAT: Legendary hermit of Providence

WHERE: East Providence

COST: Free

PRO TIP: Robert's home was said to be near the bridge from Fox Point to Bold Point in East Providence, on the Watchemoket Farm property owned by Tristam Burgess.

Robert the Hermit (New York Public Libraries Digital Collection)

ROBERT THE HERMIT

its florid title—*The Life and Adventures of Robert, the Hermit of Massachusetts, Who has Lived 14 Years in a Cave, Secluded from Human Society: Comprising, an Account of his Birth, Parentage, Sufferings, and Providential Escape from Unjust and Cruel Bondage in Early Life*, and *His Reasons for Becoming a Recluse*—the story of Robert the Hermit became an influential tract for the antislavery movement in the years leading up to the Civil War.

Another Rhode Island hermit, Arnold Sherman, lived in a hut near Curtis Corner Road in West Kingston along the Narragansett Pier Railway tracks and shunned human contact for 25 years until his death in 1897.

SECRET SPRAY

Where was the technology developed that allows planes to fight at night?

The Beavertail Lighthouse in Jamestown is one of Rhode Island's most popular tourist destinations, but practically in the shadow of the 64-foot lighthouse overlooking Narragansett Bay are the remains of one of the most top-secret research facilities of World War II.

Hiking trails on the north end of Beavertail State Park lead along the beautiful and rugged coastal cliffs of Conanicut Island, but also to something unusual. In the woods you'll come across what seems to be a paved trail, but is actually the old access road to the Spraycliff Observatory and the former Naval Radio Station Jamestown.

The naval station had an array of large radio towers for sending and receiving messages from shore to ships at sea. The Spraycliff Observatory, on the other hand, performed a critical, top-secret task: developing and testing radar compact enough that it could be installed on fighter aircraft.

BEAVERTAIL STATE PARK

WHAT: Top-secret World War II research lab

WHERE: Beavertail State Park, Beavertail Rd., Jamestown

COST: Free

PRO TIP: Take the Red Trail from the northwest parking lot at Beavertail to access the former Spraycliff property.

Modern radar was developed prior to the war, but required bulky equipment to operate, so researchers at Spraycliff worked with new technology to perfect radar equipment for night fighters, which previously were literally flying blind on most missions to intercept attacking enemy planes in the dark.

Code-named Project Affirm, the quest to develop night-fighter radar for use against Japanese aircraft in the Pacific

Top: Corsair fighter planes at Quonset Point (US Navy/public domain)

Inset: Hiking trail to Spraycliff site

included testing the experimental gear from the Spraycliff Observatory on aircraft based at the nearby Quonset Naval Air Station. By August 1943, the first radar-equipped squadron of Chance-Vought Corsair night fighters was in action, busily shooting down the Japanese "Washing Machine Charley" planes (so named for the unusual sound of their engines) that had been harassing US ground troops every night for months on Guadalcanal and other island battlefields.

ELITE ANIMALS

Why do exotic animals roam the grounds of an estate in Newport?

Multimillion-dollar homes compete for the eye's attention along the posh Ocean Drive in Newport, but there's only one where you might see a Cotswold sheep or Ancient White Park cattle staring back.

When wealthy copper and railroad speculator Arthur Curtis James founded the Surprise Valley Farm on Harrison Avenue in the early 1900s, part of his vision was to re-create a Swiss style farm with a barn to house his herd of rare Guernsey cattle. Dubbed the "Swiss Village" by locals, the unique and beautiful gentleman's farm raised a variety of animals over the years; later, the grounds were used for an addiction treatment program and as a training facility for people with disabilities.

In 1998, however, the Swiss Village returned to its roots and once again began operating as a farm, again with some unusual inhabitants. The Swiss Village Foundation acquired a total of 45 acres of prime Newport real estate with the mission of conserving heritage breeds of livestock, like Ancient White Park cattle (possibly introduced to England by the Romans), Oberhasli goats from Switzerland, and St. Croix sheep, descendants of African breeds brought on slave ships to the US Virgin Islands.

OCEAN HOUR FARM

WHAT: Farm full of rare animals in ritzy Newport

WHERE: 152 Harrison Ave., Newport

COST: Free

PRO TIP: Ocean Hour Farm is affiliated with 11th Hour Racing, a competitive sailing team that works to protect and restore the world's oceans.

Heritage breed sheep grazing at Ocean Hour Farm (Ocean Hour Farm)

While rolling, rocky fields around the historic farm buildings are populated with farm critters rather than millionaires, the mission of the foundation went beyond animal husbandry. In partnership with Tufts University's Cummings School of Veterinary Medicine, the group collected and froze seeds and reproductive material from rare and endangered food plants and animals to preserve them for future generations. In 2022, the farm was acquired by a local philanthropist and its mission changed to one of sustainability, but the owners of the new Ocean Hour Farm have pledged to continue nurturing the herds of rare animals.

THE UNFORGETTABLE FIRE

Where is one of the worst nightclub fires in US history remembered?

Hundreds of rock music fans gathered on a frigid night in February 2003 at the Station nightclub in West Warwick to hear the band Great White perform. As the show opened, pyrotechnics lit behind the band ignited flammable soundproofing material around the stage. The fire quickly flashed over the crowded building, and within minutes the room was engulfed in thick, black smoke.

The crowd rushed to escape the fire, but some people were trampled in the panic and others could not find the side exits. Many instinctively made for the door they had entered in the front of the building, but a zizagging entryway made exiting difficult. The surge of people quickly led to the door being blocked. Overcome by toxic smoke, many people died just feet from the door.

In total, what became known as the Station Fire killed 100 people and injured many more, some with horrific burns. Investigators found a number of factors that contributed to the tragedy, including the use of flammable foam as sound insulation, the lack of a sprinkler system in the building, and the poor design of the front door area.

Park entrance and memorial

After the fire, the gutted remains of the nightclub were bulldozed, and the property quickly became the site of informal memorials to the victims. The Station Fire Memorial Foundation eventually acquired the property via donation by the owner, and in 2017 a $2 million memorial to those who died in the fourth-worst nightclub fire in US history was dedicated.

Located at 211 Cowesett Avenue, the memorial park is open to the public and includes walking paths, gardens, and a stone pavilion. Circular monuments, engraved with symbols resembling old 45-rpm record adapters, are surrounded by markers with the names and images of those who died.

EGG ROLLS AND JAZZ

How did a Chinese restaurant become one of Rhode Island's top live music venues?

Chan's restaurant in downtown Woonsocket is about as old-school as Chinese restaurants get. Established in 1905, its menu is full of the kind of Chinese food that has been popular with Americans for more than a century, like egg foo yong and beef lo mein.

What really makes Chan's stand out, however, is not what's on the menu but what's on the restaurant's calendar, which is filled with a regular schedule of live blues, rock, and jazz music.

John Chan, owner of Chan's Fine Oriental Dining, grew up working in his father's restaurant and, after graduating Providence College, took over the business and saw the potential to add a performance space in the restaurant's large dining room. Now in its fourth decade, the 130-seat Chan's Four Seasons Jazz and Blues Club—less formally known as "Chan's Egg Rolls and Jazz"—has attracted most of the top performers in New England at one time or another.

CHAN'S FINE ORIENTAL DINING

WHAT: Legendary live music performed in a Chinese restaurant

WHERE: 267 Main St., Woonsocket

COST: Free

PRO TIP: The Stadium Theater is another great venue for live music in downtown Woonsocket.

Dizzy Gillespie, Leon Redbone, James Montgomery, Duke Robillard, Roomful of Blues, Sugar Ray, and Commander Cody all have played Chan's, which also has hosted movie premiere events for the Farrelly brothers' *There's Something about Mary* and *Stuck on You*, karaoke, and a monthly open-mike night for emerging artists.

Guitarist JD Simo playing at Chan's

While live jazz was the focus early on, Chan's quickly added other types of acts and artists to the lineup, which now includes comedians, original rock groups, and tribute bands playing the music of Led Zeppelin, the Doors, and more. All the tasty tunes are served with a side of Cantonese, Szechuan, Hunan, Mandarin, and Shanghai cuisine.

MALL RATS

How did a group of artists spend years secretly living in a Providence shopping mall?

When the Providence Place Mall opened in 1999, it was hailed as a cornerstone of the revival of the retail landscape in downtown Providence. But while the mall is packed with stores, restaurants, and even an IMAX theater, one thing that the developers never intended was for it to have residents.

A group of Providence artists, however, had their own plans. Over a four-year span, Michael Townshend, Adriana Young, and several other people shared a 750-square-foot apartment that they carved out of an unused and overlooked space in the mall's parking garage.

The group lived rent-free, albeit illegally, above a storage room, building a wall of concrete blocks for added privacy and sprucing up the room with couches, tables, chairs, and other furniture. The apartment lacked running water and a toilet (residents used mall bathrooms), but an extension cord plugged into a forgotten outlet provided electricity.

Townshend had noticed the unused space when jogging past the mall when it was under construction, and envisioned the living arrangement as a quasi-art installation. Mall officials, however, were not amused when he was caught in 2007, and

THE PROVIDENCE PLACE MALL

WHAT: Secret mall apartment

WHERE: Providence Place Mall, Providence Pl., Providence

COST: Free

PRO TIP: The first indoor shopping mall in the US, the Providence Arcade on Weybosset St. in Providence, has taken an opposite tack. After nearly two centuries as a retail center, it now has been converted into microloft apartments.

The Providence Place Mall

charged Townshend with trespassing and banned him from the property for life.

The arrest not only ended the apartment dwellers' unauthorized stint as mall residents, but also thwarted their ambitious plans to improve the place with wood flooring and plumbing. The apartment was dismantled, and the secret entrance used by the residents locked up, but their long-running residency in the bowels of the luxury mall has become the stuff of postmodern Providence legend.

The same group of artists who lived in the mall were also involved in an earlier art installation in a forgotten storm drain in Providence.

SHOTS THROUGH THE DORR

Why was an armed revolt launched against the Rhode Island government in 1842?

The American Revolution didn't bring democracy to Rhode Island. Despite the promises of the Declaration of Independence and the federal Constitution, Rhode Island continued to operate under a 1663 royal charter as its governing document, which stipulated that only property owners had the right to vote.

By the 1840s, middle-class citizens like Thomas Dorr of Chepachet were fed up with the disenfranchisement, which put most of the power in the state in the hands of rural landowners. Dorr was elected governor of Rhode Island in 1842, but the sitting governor, Samuel Ward King, refused to step down. After failing to change the voting system legislatively, Dorr and his allies gathered armed forces in the village of Chepachet; King, in turn, ordered the state militia to confront Dorr.

Seeking to avoid bloodshed, Dorr disbanded his forces and fled the state. The short-lived revolt was ultimately successful, however. Later that year, the state legislature adopted a new constitution that expanded voting rights to non-landowners.

Cemetery Hill on US Route 44 in Chepachet is where Dorr assembled his forces, and the Tavern on Main building just down the road at 1157 Putnam Pike—then Sprague's Tavern—was intended as the site for Dorr's legislature to

TAVERN ON MAIN

WHAT: Dorr Rebellion tavern

WHERE: Tavern on Main, 1157 Putnam Pike, Chepachet

COST: Free

PRO TIP: The Pettingill-Mason House at 1043 Putnam Pike is home to a Dorr Rebellion exhibit by the Glocester Heritage Society.

Top: *Tavern on Main, Chepachet*

Inset: *Thomas Dorr*

assemble. Instead, King's forces shot their way into the building and ended up occupying the tavern for months in order to quell the rebellion. Stop in at the second-oldest tavern in Rhode Island for a taste of this forgotten history, and perhaps an encounter with Dorr himself—the building is said to be haunted.

ANIMAL ART

Where do artists find inspiration in stuffed animals?

If you want to learn how to draw or sculpt an animal or plant, it helps to have one handy to examine and interpret. And that's the whole idea behind the Nature Lab at the Rhode Island School of Design (RISD), a little-known (other than by RISD students) collection of natural history specimens that has been informing the work of aspiring artists since 1937.

Founded by and named for RISD faculty member Edna Lawrence, the Nature Lab is a mix of the decidedly old-school—stuffed bears, birds, and blowfish—and cutting-edge resources, like three-dimensional images of the collection's more than 80,000 items of flora and fauna. With its mounted animal heads and desiccated skulls filling walls of glass display cases, the Nature Lab resembles a 19th-century museum, but is more dynamic than dry—the collection also includes live specimens of plants, small animals, and fish gathered from Narragansett Bay.

EDNA LAWRENCE NATURE LAB

WHAT: Taxidermic inspiration for artists

WHERE: 13 Waterman St., Providence

COST: Free

PRO TIP: You can view the fruits of the Nature Lab's animal inspiration at RISD's Chace Center (20 N Main St.), which includes access to the RISD Museum and galleries of student work.

Many of the specimens available at the RISD Nature Lab were gathered by founder Edna Lawrence during her travels around the world.

RISD Nature Lab (Rhode Island School of Design)

Students are permitted hands-on access to items that inspire their work, which extends to microscopic objects useful for visualizing naturally occurring patterns and structures. Access to the general public, however, is limited to occasional tours and visits by appointment only.

THE BATTLE OF RHODE ISLAND

Where did a regiment of Black soldiers make a heroic stand during the American Revolution?

Rhode Island has just one historic battlefield, but the Revolutionary War's Battle of Rhode Island is barely remembered, probably because the clash of arms was inconclusive and was quickly followed by a retreat by the Americans. But the battle in August of 1778 was notable for the role that the 1st Rhode Island Regiment—a unit of Black and Native American soldiers—played in repulsing an attack by British forces.

Great Britain had occupied Newport and much of Aquidneck Island since 1776 but, bolstered by a French naval force, the Continental Army led by Major General John Sullivan crossed by boat from the mainland and laid siege to Newport two years later. When the French fleet suddenly departed, however, the Americans decided to withdraw; deserters informed the British in Newport, who then launched an attack on Sullivan's lines of defense, which stretched across Aquidneck Island in Portsmouth.

PATRIOTS PARK

WHAT: History of a mostly forgotten Revolutionary War battle

WHERE: State Rte. 114 in Portsmouth, just south of the Rte. 24 S overpass

COST: Free

PRO TIP: The grounds of the Portsmouth Historical Society museum at 870 E Main Rd. include a monument marking the site of an ambush of British forces by American troops early in the Battle of Rhode Island.

114

Left: Black Regiment monument at Patriots Park

Right: Butts Hill fortifications

During the battle, Hessian soldiers under British command attacked the right flank of the American lines but were driven back three times by the 1st Rhode Island Regiment. Elsewhere, the back-and-forth battle with British forces confronting Continental Army and state militia troops entrenched on Turkey Hill and Quaker Hill ended indecisively. Afterward, the American forces conducted an orderly retreat from Aquidneck Island.

Parts of the site of the Battle of Rhode Island are preserved at Patriots Park in Portsmouth, a National Historic Landmark, which also includes a monument to the 1st Rhode Island Regiment, which was one of the few units to serve throughout the entire Revolutionary War. Nearby Butts Hill served as a fortified command post for the American forces, and the earthworks on the hill—the largest such fortification in southern New England—still are visible.

HORSE SOLDIERS

**Where was Narragansett Park, and why
did it need to be guarded with machine guns?**

Rhode Island is hardly a stranger to bare-knuckle politics, but it usually doesn't involve a declaration of martial law.

In the 1930s and 1940s, Narragansett Park in Pawtucket was one of the most famous horse racing venues in America: Seabiscuit won his first race here, and in 1942 the track hosted a legendary match race between Triple Crown winner Whirlaway and Preakness Stakes winner Alshab (which won by a nose in a dramatic finish).

That was nothing, however, compared to the butting of heads between track president Walter O'Hara and Rhode Island Governor Robert E. Quinn in 1937. After Quinn accused O'Hara of interfering with the state racing steward, O'Hara implied that Quinn should be locked up in the psychiatric ward at Butler Hospital in Providence. Quinn then ordered that O'Hara be removed as president of the track, and suspended his operating license.

When the racecourse failed to close as ordered at the end of the summer season, O'Hara declared the facility to be in a state of insurrection and called out the Rhode Island National Guard to seize the property. Soldiers armed with machine guns were stationed at the gates; in response, a defiant O'Hara played "March of the Wooden Soldiers" over the track's public address system.

NARRAGANSETT PARK

WHAT: Once-famous racecourse

WHERE: 645 Narragansett Park Dr., Pawtucket

COST: Free

PRO TIP: Streets on the former grounds of the racetrack are named for horses that ran there, including Whirlaway Place and Seabiscuit Place.

Narragansett Park (Providence Public Library)

O'Hara eventually resigned, but Quinn's political career suffered due to public ridicule over the "Race Track War" and the large cost of stationing the National Guard at the track. Narragansett Park closed in 1978 after years of decline. The former grandstand of the park was converted into a discount retail store called Building #19 and still stands, but is currently unoccupied.

Red Pollard, the famous jockey of Seabiscuit and a Pawtucket resident, is buried in Notre Dame Cemetery, about a mile from the track.

CIVIC SUDS

Why does the town of Narragansett greet visitors with an old beer sign?

Narragansett is a seaside community known for its beautiful beaches and its landmark Towers, an elegant remnant of a grand casino and hotel that once stood at the edge of Narragansett Pier. So why does the welcome sign at the gateway to town have roots in something as prosaic as a brewery?

The Narragansett Brewing Company was founded in 1890, not in Narragansett but in Cranston. The flagship Narragansett lager became the favorite regional beer of New England, with the brewery sponsoring the Boston Red Sox radio broadcasts and Robert Shaw's Captain Quint famously crushing a can of 'Gansett against his head in *Jaws*. However, the company fell on hard times and shut down its Cranston brewery in 1981.

A group of Rhode Islanders purchased the brand in 2005, and Narragansett beer can once again be found in bars and "packies" everywhere in the state. The revival came too late for the old brewery, which was demolished in 1998. However, former Narragansett town council president Ted ("Mr. Narragansett") Wright was able to salvage the sign that once adorned the brewery building, relocating the familiar script to a brick sign in the middle of the Dillon Rotary at the entrance to town.

NARRAGANSETT ROTARY

WHAT: Narragansett welcome sign

WHERE: Rotary at intersection of State routes 108 and 1A in Narragansett

COST: Free

PRO TIP: In addition to Narragansett lager, the revived Narragansett Brewery leans heavily into its Rhode Island heritage with brews incorporating Del's Lemonade, Autocrat Coffee Syrup, and Allie's Donuts.

Narragansett welcome sign

It's a fitting symbol of welcome—after all, Narragansett's famous slogan, then and now, is "Hi, Neighbor!" And while the town of Narragansett still doesn't have a brewery of its own, the current owners of Narragansett beer recently opened a new brewery and beer hall at Providence's India Point Park.

Springfield, Massachusetts, native Theodor Seuss Geisel, better known as Dr. Seuss, was one of many artists who illustrated ads hawking Narragansett Beer.

PUNKED PROCESSION

Where can you enjoy a procession devoted entirely to mockery?

If you want to enjoy a typical Fourth of July parade with marching bands, fire trucks, and cheerleaders, head to Bristol, which hosts the nation's longest-running Independence Day celebration. But if you would rather spend the day indulging in that other great American tradition—mocking politicians and other public figures—the Ancients and Horribles Parade in Glocester delivers the kind of hilarious fireworks you'll enjoy.

A satirical take on processions honoring "ancient and honorable" civic organizations, Ancients and Horribles parades were once fairly common in New England, but the Glocester march—founded in 1926—is one of the few remaining.

If the Fourth of July got drunk and hooked up with a Mardi Gras krewe, the Ancients and Horribles parade would be their love child. Costumed marchers and float inhabitants run the gamut from the simply weird (people dressed up as Raggedy Ann dolls, superheroes, and Elvis) to protests against GMOs

ANCIENTS AND HORRIBLES PARADE

WHAT: Mocking parade where nothing is sacred

WHERE: Main St., Chepachet

COST: Free

PRO TIP: More of a doer than a watcher? Anyone is welcome to march in the parade, and you can register right up until the day of the event.

The village of Wickford in North Kingstown also has a Horribles Parade, but it's a Halloween costume parade and mostly absent of satire.

*Float in the Ancients and Horribles parade
(Blackstone Valley Tourism Council)*

and a proposed local power plant and odes to beloved but departed local stores.

The greatest ire is saved for state, local, and national politicians. Political leaders are welcome to join the parade (actually, pretty much anyone can), and some bravely do. But they're just as likely to be greeted by a manure truck carrying their images down the main street of Chepachet as they are to applause from the crowd lining the road.

YANKEE DOODLE DADDY

Who was the Fox Point kid credited with "creating" Broadway?

George M. Cohan, born in Providence on July 4, 1878, may have been destined to write "Yankee Doodle Dandy," but the legendary song and dance man accomplished far more during his life than penning one patriotic song. Cohan also was a vaudeville actor, producer, director, and writer of more than 40 plays. Other timeless tunes penned by Cohen include "It's a Grand Old Flag" and "Over There," the latter the anthem of American soldiers serving in Europe during World War I.

Dubbed the "Man Who Created Broadway," Cohan was a legend in his own time, becoming the first artist to receive the Congressional Gold Medal in 1936. After his death in 1942, Cohan was honored with a statue in the heart of Times Square with the inscription "Give my regards to Broadway" carved on the base.

Nor was Cohan's status as a local boy done good forgotten back in Rhode Island. A jaunty bust of Cohan by artist Robert Shure was erected on July 3, 2009, at the corner of Wickenden and Governor streets in Providence, close to Cohan's birthplace in the Fox Point neighborhood. The intersection was renamed George M. Cohan Plaza, and a street in the community was named George M. Cohan Boulevard. Cohan's birthplace at 536 Wickenden Street was razed to make way for the Boys and Girls Club of Providence, but many

GEORGE M. COHAN MONUMENT

WHAT: Fox Point's most famous son

WHERE: Intersection of Wickenden and Governor Streets, Providence

COST: Free

PRO TIP: Pop into Round Again Records at 278 Wickenden St. to look for Broadway music on vinyl.

Left: George M. Cohan monument

Right: George M. Cohan (Library of Congress)

of the other buildings on the street remain as they were in the Broadway legend's youth.

THE PIRATES RETIREMENT HOME

What Jamestown estate was once home to an infamous buccaneer?

Thomas Paine was the rare pirate who dodged bullets, swords, and the gallows long enough to enjoy a peaceful retirement, although his past followed him to his country home in Jamestown, sparking tales of buried booty.

Officially, Paine was a privateer, commissioned by the governor of Jamaica to attack pirates. Unofficially, he sometimes engaged in piracy himself, raiding the Spanish city of St. Augustine, Florida, in 1683 and also looting towns in Colombia and Venezuela. Closer to home, Paine led a successful mission to evict a group of French privateers from Block Island.

Paine became a popular hero in Rhode Island after driving off the French, and he settled down into a quiet life in Jamestown, becoming a respectable pillar of the community. He parlayed some of his privateering money into building a house on the east coast of Conanicut Island, calling it Cajacet. It was here in 1699 that he received an unexpected visit from an old friend, William Kidd. The infamous Captain Kidd was on the run from local authorities and seeking help and a hiding place for a cargo of gold, which he hoped could fund his defense against charges of piracy. Ultimately, the visit

CAJACET FARM

WHAT: Jamestown pirate house

WHERE: 850 E Shore Rd., Jamestown

COST: Free

PRO TIP: The Jamestown Historical Society museum at 92 Narragansett Ave. has more information about Thomas Paine.

Top: Jamestown pirate house (Mott & Chace Sotheby's International Realty)

Inset: Captain William Kidd

did Kidd no good: he was convicted of piracy and hung in London in 1701.

Legend holds that Kidd gave some of his treasure to Paine, and that it may still be buried somewhere on Jamestown. Paine died in 1715, but Cajacet still stands at 850 East Shore Road in Jamestown. The Cajacet Farm property includes the expanded but recognizable house that Paine built in 1690. It's still a private residence, so you can't visit; your best opportunity to catch a glimpse of the house is—appropriately enough—from a boat in Narragansett Bay. As for that buried treasure, you're welcome to search for it on the beaches of Jamestown, all of which are public property up to the mean high-tide line.

125

FAMILY GUY

Where in the heck is Quahog, Rhode Island?

The famously irreverent comedy *Family Guy* may be a cartoon, but it's set in a real place . . . well, kinda-sorta. Peter Griffin and family live in Rhode Island, which seems pretty random until you remember that series creator Seth MacFarlane is a graduate of the Rhode Island School of Design and lived in the Ocean State for several years, or at least long enough to soak up some of the state's quirks.

The show reveals the Griffin family's home address—31 Spooner Street in Quahog, Rhode Island—but while there's a Spooner Street in Providence, there's no town called Quahog (which is actually a type of clam indigenous to Rhode Island that can be found in the local chowder). MacFarlane has said that Quahog is based on Cranston, which makes sense considering that you can in fact see the Providence skyline from many parts of this suburban city, just as in the show.

QUAHOG, RI

WHAT: *Family Guy*'s Rhode Island roots

WHERE: Various locations

COST: Free

PRO TIP: The three real buildings that appear in every *Family Guy* episode as the background for the Griffin home are the Hospital Trust Tower, the Fleet Center, and the Industrial Trust Tower, better known as the Superman Building.

Family Guy creator Seth MacFarlane got his start in cartoons when a professor at the Rhode Island School of Design submitted his thesis film to animation studio Hanna-Barbera.

Top: The Providence skyline that appears in every episode of Family Guy

Inset: Greetings from Quahog postcard

Rhode Island visitors might not run into Stewie, Meg, Lois, Chris, or Brian on the streets of Quahog, or meet Peter and Glenn Quagmire for a mug of Pawtucket Patriot beer at the Drunken Clam (neither of which actually exist), but there are a host of actual Rhode Island landmarks that have been featured in the show. The Blackstone Valley Tourism Council put together a *Family Guy* tour map for Rhode Island ComicCon a few years back, which includes stops at sites like the Van Wickle Gates at Brown University, the Modern Diner in Pawtucket, Wes' Rib House in Providence, the Big Blue Bug statue, and Wright's Chicken Farm.

A TREE GROWS IN BRISTOL

Why does little Rhody have such big trees?

You don't have to hop a flight to the West Coast to see a giant redwood tree: the tallest *Sequoiadendron giganteum* east of the Mississippi spreads its mighty branches at the waterfront Blithewold Mansion, Gardens, and Arboretum in Bristol.

Better known as giant sequoia, these trees definitely live up to their name. They are the most massive plants on earth—some weigh more than 2,000 tons—and can grow more than 300 feet tall and live more than 3,000 years.

The giant sequoia at Blithewold is a baby by comparison. Planted in 1930, it stands about 110 feet tall in the enclosed garden at the Bristol arboretum. The tree was a gift to former Blithewold owner Marjorie Lyon from landscape architect John DeWolf, who acquired it from the greenhouse at Prospect Park in New York. Giant sequoia are native only to parts of the Sierra Nevada mountains in California, but Rhode Island is at a similar latitude and, when the tree was planted, had a cool, foggy climate in coastal areas like Bristol that was not unlike the Sequoia's usual domain. The climate has warmed considerably since then, however, putting the tree under considerable stress.

BLITHEWOLD ARBORETUM

WHAT: Rhode Island redwood trees

WHERE: Blithewold Arboretum, 101 Ferry Rd. (State Rte. 114), Bristol

COST: Adults: $16; Children 6-17: $6

PRO TIP: Tickets include access to both the gardens and the historic Blithewold Mansion, where a traditional tea and scones service is offered seasonally.

Giant sequoia at Blithewold (Blithewold Arboretum)

The "big mama" tree isn't the only giant sequoia in Bristol. Concerned about hurricanes damaging her prized redwood, Lyon cultivated a number of seedlings from the original giant sequoia and planted them elsewhere in her gardens, and gave seedlings to other Bristol residents. Among the arboretum's extensive collection of rare and large trees is also a massive dawn redwood (*Metasequoia glyptostroboides*), a Chinese redwood that can top 100 feet tall.

129

CLINGING SHINGLES

Why is the most famous house in Narragansett Bay shingled both inside and out?

There's no more intriguing house in Rhode Island than Clingstone, a three-story cottage built in 1905 on a rocky outcrop in Narragansett Bay known as the Dumplings. If you hate mowing your lawn, Clingstone is the home for you: the house takes up almost all of the available surface area of the bare, wave-scoured rocks.

Owner J. S. Lovering Wharton built the house off Bull Point in Jamestown as a summer home, but Clingstone also was uncomfortably close to the coastal defense battery at Fort Wetherall. As the story goes, Wharton decided to shingle the interior of the house as well as the exterior, because he was concerned that the frequent cannon fire by the US Army Coast Artillery Corps would shake the plaster off of his walls.

The house perches as precariously above the bay as its name suggests, but nonetheless it rode out both the fierce 1938 hurricane and 1954's Hurricane Carol. After being abandoned for decades, it was purchased in 1961 by architect Henry Wood.

Now renovated and powered by solar panels, Clingstone is available as a pricey weekly rental property. In addition to isolation and million-dollar views of Narragansett Bay, a stay at Clingstone includes the opportunity to examine up close the house's unique shingled walls, some of which are embedded with marbles shot into the

CLINGSTONE

WHAT: A house on a rock

WHERE: The Dumplings, Narragansett Bay

COST: $8,000 a week to rent

PRO TIP: The best views of Clingstone are from a boat on the bay, Old Salt Work Beach in Jamestown, or Ft. Adams in Newport.

Clingstone

wood by vandals who invaded the home during the years that it stood unoccupied.

Patience Island in Narragansett Bay is much larger than the Dumplings, but also has just one house. The address is 0 Patience Way.

TROUBLED TEMPLE

Why did it take 80 years to open a classically designed building in Providence?

Freemasonry is a celebration of skilled construction, so it's perhaps the height of irony that a majestic building designed to house the Freemasons of Rhode Island was abandoned midconstruction in 1928 and sat vacant for decades before finally being reborn as a luxury hotel.

Fronted by a classic Ionic colonnade and clad in limestone, Providence's Masonic Temple was conceived as a meeting hall and office space on the shoulder of Smith Hill, home of the equally elegant Rhode Island State House. Work on the 155,000-square-foot building commenced in 1926, but workers walked out of the project when money for construction dried up in 1928.

The shell of the building sat sadly empty in the heart of Providence until well into the 21st century, even as a companion structure was purchased and finished by the state of Rhode Island, opening as the Rhode Island Veterans Memorial Auditorium in 1951. The auditorium and the Masonic Temple were listed on the National Register of Historic Places in 1993, but it wasn't until 2007 that construction on the temple building was finally finished. Purchased by a hotel developer, the building reopened as the Renaissance Providence Downtown Hotel, taking advantage of

THE PROVIDENCE MASONIC TEMPLE

WHAT: Monumental never-finished lodge building

WHERE: Renaissance Providence Hotel, 5 Ave. of the Arts, Providence

COST: Rooms from $215 per night

PRO TIP: Commissioned graffiti art in the hotel's basement restaurant is a nod to the temple's long period of neglect and abandonment.

The Renaissance Providence Downtown Hotel

a prime location between the State House and the recently opened Providence Place Mall.

The hotel retains the temple's Greek Revival facade and also pays tribute to the building's history with Masonic architectural flourishes in the foyer and lobby. Freemasonry symbols are worked into the decor and artwork, and the blueprints for the original temple are displayed on the lobby wall.

BAD BOYS

Where can you shop and dine on the grounds of a former boys reform school?

If you think that the Chapel View shopping center in Cranston looks a little overbuilt, you're not wrong. Nobody starts out saying that they're going to raise a string of three-story stone cottages to house a Cold Stone Creamery and a Massage Envy.

Where kids lick ice cream cones and adults get their knots worked out was, up until the 1980s, a much more somber place. The buildings were part of the Sockanosset School for Boys, a reform school built in 1881 and still housing wayward youth as recently as 1985, when it finally shut down for good. A combination juvenile detention facility and reformatory, the school neighbored the state prison (built in 1878, and still in operation) and included classrooms, residential dormitories (now the retail buildings), a superintendent's home, gym, infirmary, and a chapel.

At first, the boys from "broken or badly bent" homes who were sentenced to Sockanosset spent their days working on farms and performing other physical labor; later, classroom education and vocational training was added in a machine shop, carpenter shop, print shop, mason shop, and a blacksmith shop. Residents cooked their own food and maintained the facilities.

SOCKANOSSET SCHOOL FOR BOYS

WHAT: Former reform school turned shopping center

WHERE: Chapel View Blvd. (off State Rte. 2), Cranston

COST: Free

PRO TIP: Generations of Rhode Islanders warned their unruly children that if they didn't behave, they'd be shipped off to "Socko" or the "Training School."

Former chapel of the Sockanosset School for Boys

The dormitory buildings, although built for an unromantic purpose, remain visually arresting, but the best way to immerse in the atmosphere of the old reform school is to visit its former chapel, which has been converted into the upscale Chapel Grille restaurant. Built in 1891, the chapel building now is the bar area of the hotel, and you can admire the stained-glass windows, exposed stone walls, timbered roof, and choir balcony while sipping an Angel Martini and dining on Mediterranean and Italian food.

GAME ROOM WITH A VIEW

Where can you find a penny arcade deep in the woods of Rhode Island?

Spring Lake in Burrillville is a typical country watering hole, a modest community beach where residents of rural Rhode Island can cool off or catch some rays without having to make the long trip down to the shore. But there's one thing at Spring Lake that's truly exceptional, and well worth the price of a few dollars' admission to the beach, and that's its fantastic beachside arcade.

Established in 1930 to entertain beachgoers and provide rainy-day diversions, the Spring Lake Arcade bills itself as the oldest penny arcade in America. You can still play games here for a penny, though some cost a nickel, dime, or even the princely sum of a quarter. A few games date back to the 1920s, including peepshow machines displaying vintage cartoons, and there are also electromechanical car and horse racing games from the 1930s and 1940s, shooting galleries, decades' worth of pinball machines, and a smattering of more modern video games.

As lake beaches go, Spring Lake is a lot of fun, even without the arcade. There's a broad swath of sand to spread

SPRING LAKE ARCADE

WHAT: Vintage arcade at a town beach

WHERE: 52 Old Hillside Dr., Burrillville

COST: Beach admission is $5 for Burrillville residents, $7 for nonresidents

PRO TIP: For a modern take on the classic arcade, check out the Free Play arcade bar at 182 Pine St. in Providence, which has dozens of video games, pinball machines, and table games like air hockey and Skee-Ball.

Games at the Spring Lake Arcade (Paul Kandarian)

out on, the lake water is clean and cool, and concessions include a snack bar and boat rentals. The beach and arcade are open from June to early September.

Another place to play cool old arcade games is the Electromagnetic Pinball Museum and Restoration in Pawtucket, which has a collection of working, predigital pinball machines.

BUS LINE

Where did students once ride the rails to class in converted school buses?

The Narragansett Pier Railroad had an interesting run. Established in 1876 as a spur line off of the main New York, Providence, and Boston Railroad, the railroad went just eight miles from Kingston Station to Narragansett Pier. It was built to bring people from New York and Boston to the resort community in Narragansett, where they would connect to steamships that would take the Gilded Age travelers onward to Newport.

For a short time, both passenger trains and electric trolleys operated along the line. Business declined as the automobile took over, and scheduled passenger service ended in 1952. But not before a fascinating period when local schoolchildren and other passengers rode the rails on gasoline-powered school buses between West Kingston and Narragansett. The buses, nicknamed "Mickey Dinks" after their two drivers, Mickey Redmond and "Dink" Gould, operated from the 1920s to the 1950s.

The Narragansett Pier Railroad hung on as a freight line until the early 1980s, despite twice shortening the length of its route. Decades after the railroad shut down, most of the railbed was converted into a rail trail, the William C. O'Neill Bike Path (aka the South County Bike Path). The paved, multiuse

WILLIAM C. O'NEILL BIKE PATH

WHAT: Former Narragansett Pier Railroad

WHERE: South Kingstown and Narragansett

COST: Free

PRO TIP: It's not on the bike path, but the terminal building for the Narragansett Pier Railroad still stands at 145 Boon St. in Narragansett.

Top: The William C. O'Neill Bike Path

Inset: Mickey Dinks bus

trail runs seven miles, from Kingston Station to Narragansett, with another one-mile segment planned in order to bring the path right to the shore at Narragansett Beach. The route includes a number of remnants of the old railroad, including the former Peach Dale station building on Railroad Street, one of the only on-road segments of the path.

HOT POTATOES

Why are visitors to the Lake Mishnock fire station greeted by a giant spud?

There are many icons associated with firefighting—fire trucks, dalmatians, hoses, axes—but suffice it to say that a potato isn't one of them. So it's strange, indeed, that the mascot at the Lake Mishnock Fire Department, on Mishnock Road in West Greenwich, is a six-foot potato wearing a firefighter's helmet and yellow bunker pants and wielding a pike.

The fire department doesn't have some unusual love for spuds: the mascot actually is one of 37 Mr. Potato Head statues built by Rhode Island–based toy company Hasbro in 2000 and placed in various sites around the state. Created as part of a tourism marketing campaign, the statues were—like the toy itself—customized to fit various themes. There was the firefighter Potato Head at Lake Mishnock, a surfer dude Potato Head for Narragansett, an Uncle Sam Potato Head for Bristol, and more.

The statues got a lot of publicity at first, but interest in the gimmick soon waned, along with the era when seemingly every tourist community was populating its streets with fiberglass horses, frogs, and other symbols of civic pride. Over the years, some of the potatoes were vandalized, while others were harvested by private collectors.

MR. POTATO HEAD STATUES

WHAT: Themed spuds sown around Rhode Island

WHERE: Lake Mishnock, Fire Department and other locations

COST: Free

PRO TIP: Also located on Mishnock Rd. near the fire station is the Mishnock Barn, a fish-out-of-water country-and-western bar in Rhode Island that features line dancing, dance lessons, and live music.

Firefighter Potato Head

A few survive, however. The best-tended is the handsome, original Mr. Potato Head outside the Hasbro company building on Newport Avenue in Pawtucket. Firefighter Potato Head at Lake Mishnock also is reasonably well cared for, and Uncle Sam Potato Head gets buffed up and wheeled out (on a flatbed truck) for the annual Bristol Fourth of July parade. You also can eye a few other hardy tubers at the Westerly Airport, Clements Marketplace in Portsmouth, the Day-O-Lite factory in Warwick, and behind the Glocester Town Hall in Chepachet—the latter honoring Betty the Learned Elephant.

AVENUE ARTS

How did Providence get all those giant (and Giant) murals?

Providence likes to think of itself as the cultural capital of Rhode Island in addition to being the actual state capital, and it doesn't take too much time walking downtown to understand where that notion arises. In addition to being a premier center for the visual (Rhode Island School of Design) and culinary (Johnson & Wales University) arts, Providence is a literal palette for monumental public artworks.

Dozens of large murals cover the walls of buildings downtown. Some are by famous artists like Shepard Fairey, the RISD grad who designed the Barack Obama Hope poster as well as the Andre the Giant–inspired Obey Giant symbology. Fairey painted the *Providence Industrial* mural on Aborn Street and another social-justice-themed installation on the Founder's League Building at 91 Clemence Street. Both were done to benefit the local arts incubator AS220.

Many of the other building-sized public art in town—along with smaller works visible on utility boxes, buses, and sculpture gardens—are the visual manifestation of the mission of the Avenue Concept. Project-funded public artwork you can see includes a portrait of a young girl (*Misty Blue* by Andrew Hem) on the side wall of 118 Orange Street, Natalie Rack's *Adventure*

PROVIDENCE MURALS

WHAT: Large format public artwork

WHERE: Various locations

COST: Free

PRO TIP: The Avenue Concept's website has a tour map to more than 36 pieces of public art in and around Providence.

Downtown Providence murals

Time on the back of 94 Broad Street, and Joanna Vespia's adorable lineup of pups and kitties on the headquarters of the New England Humane Society headquarters in Cumberland.

FRENCH FRESCOES

Whose faces adorn the "Sistine Chapel of New England"?

It only takes a single glance at the twin-spired, Renaissance-style St. Ann's Catholic Church in Woonsocket to surmise that it was built to serve the city's large French Canadian population, who came to the city in the late 19th and early 20th centuries to work in the city's mills. As beautiful as the church is on the outside, however, it's what's inside the building that's truly remarkable.

Dubbed the "Sistine Chapel of New England," the church's interior is covered with hand-painted frescoes—on the walls, ceiling, transept, and chancel. Every fresco was the work of Canadian artist Guido Nincheri, who Pope Pius XI called "the church's greatest artist of religious themes." The sweeping works of art depict the stories of the Old Testament and major events in the life of Jesus Christ.

Nincheri chose church parishioners as models for his paintings, selected from the thousands of people who had made donations to fund his work. The faces of 40 of the chosen appear as angels in the 175 frescoes that Nincheri painted from 1941 to 1953.

In a weird twist of fate, Nincheri was available to work on the frescoes for such an extended period only because he had emigrated from Canada to Rhode Island after facing wartime

ST. ANN'S CATHOLIC CHURCH

WHAT: The "Sistine Chapel of America"

WHERE: 84 Cumberland St., Woonsocket

COST: Tours $10 for adults, $8 for students and seniors; free under age four.

PRO TIP: A 30-year resident of Rhode Island, Nincheri gave back to his adopted state by painting 12 other churches, as well as a series of 10 murals that now hang in the Roger Williams Park Museum.

Interior of St. Ann's Catholic Church and Cultural Center in Woonsocket

persecution by the Canadian government, largely because he had once painted a portrait of Italian dictator Benito Mussolini.

The church is now the St. Ann Arts and Cultural Center, a nonprofit community organization that hosts an annual Breakfast with the Saints and offers Sunday afternoon tours of the frescoes.

HOBBIT HOUSES

How did a piece of Middle Earth land in Richmond?

In the *Lord of the Rings*, hero Frodo Baggins and other Hobbits live in comfortable subterranean homes called "Hobbit holes," and a small village of these underground dwellings can be found in the woods of Richmond—a pet project of the chairman of the Preserve residential community and sporting club.

As a child, developer Paul Mihailides had a fascination with living underground; as an adult, he built root cellars for high-end clients. So even though he wasn't a particular fan of the J. R. R. Tolkien fantasy books or the Peter Jackson movie adaptations, he constructed his own unique version of a Hobbit House at the Preserve, dug into the earth and accessed by a heavy, round door, just like in the books and movie.

The first Hobbit House was a cozy 14 by 14 feet, warmed by a fireplace and used for intimate

THE PRESERVE SPORTING CLUB AND RESIDENCES

WHAT: *Lord of the Rings* inspired dwellings

WHERE: The Preserve Sporting Club & Residences, 87 Kingstown Rd., Richmond

COST: Event prices vary; guided tours are free for overnight guests at the Preserve.

PRO TIP: A four-course Hobbit House lunch or dinner paired with bourbon tastings costs about $181 per person for groups of four to eight.

The Preserve Sporting Club occupies 3,500 acres in Richmond—about half of a percent of the entire landmass of Rhode Island.

A Hobbit House at the Preserve

private dinners. Two larger houses later were added to create a mini Hobbiton. One, built against a natural rock wall, has cathedral ceilings inside—a virtual palace by Hobbit standards—while the newest house includes a bedroom under its thatched roof.

The houses are used for both kid-friendly and adult activities. Some privileges are for members of the Preserve only, such as overnight stays in the largest house. However, the public is invited to sign up for private Maker's Mark Hobbit House paired whiskey dinners and seasonal photo shoots.

HEAD SHOT

Why is there a cannonball embedded in a tomb at Swan Point Cemetery?

Major John Rogers Vinton was by all accounts a fine soldier—a West Point grad who saw action in the Seminole War and was honored for his gallantry during the Mexican War. So, it's a little odd that his family seemingly wanted him reminded for eternity about the proximate cause of his death in 1846.

MAJOR JOHN ROGERS VINTON GRAVE SITE

WHAT: Cannonball grave site

WHERE: Swan Point Cemetery, 585 Blackstone Blvd., Providence

COST: Free

PRO TIP: Vinton's life story is detailed in the biography *The Army Is My Calling: The Life and Writings of Major John Rogers Vinton 1801–1847* by John Missall and Mary Lou Missall.

A resident of Warren, Vinton was taking part in the battle of Vera Cruz against the Mexican Army when a cannonball ricocheted off a parapet and hit him in the head, killing him instantly. And although Vinton was an accomplished artist and devout Christian who had considered entering the ministry, his grave in Providence's Swan Point cemetery is mostly martial, flanked by cannons and topped by a cannonball.

The latter is where the story gets a little weird: the cannonball supposedly is the very one that killed Vinton.

The Battle of Veracruz, where Major John Rogers Vinton died, is considered the first successful large-scale amphibious assault in US military history.

Cannons and cannonballs adorn the grave of Major John Rogers Vinton

A military outpost in Florida, Fort Vinton, later was named for this Rhode Island soldier. Vinton is just one of the famous people interred at Swan Point Cemetery. It's also the final resting place of Major Sullivan Ballou, who died in the US Civil War shortly after writing a famously poignant letter to his wife; and horror writer H. P. Lovecraft, whose modest headstone boldly proclaims, "I Am Providence."

FIRED-UP FARM

Where can you learn about Rhode Island's steamy history in staid East Greenwich?

Steam power was one of the technological wonders of the 19th century, and many factories in the era of steam were powered by stationary engines built by Rhode Island companies like Armington & Sims, the Herreshoff Manufacturing Company, and the Corliss Steam Engine Co. A single, huge Corliss Centennial Engine powered almost all of the exhibits at the Centennial Exposition in Philadelphia in 1876, making Corliss the most famous manufacturer of steam engines in the world.

You can still see the occasional steam-powered railroad locomotive running excursion trips, but nearly all of the great steam engines that once powered American industry ended up on the scrap heap, replaced by machines powered by oil and electricity. A farm in East Greenwich is home to the only Corliss steam engine in the world that is still operational.

The 1892 Corliss Steam Engine is part of the collection at the New England Wireless & Steam Museum, which has a variety of working, steam-powered equipment, large and small, along with communications equipment dating back to the birth of wireless radio (the great-granddaddy of your cell phone, you might say). The museum is

NEW ENGLAND STEAM & WIRELESS MUSEUM

WHAT: World's only operating Corliss steam engine

WHERE: New England Wireless & Steam Museum, 1300 Frenchtown Rd., East Greenwich

COST: $10

PRO TIP: The museum's Massie Station PJ building, a National Historic Landmark, houses an intact and operational wireless transmitting station from 1907.

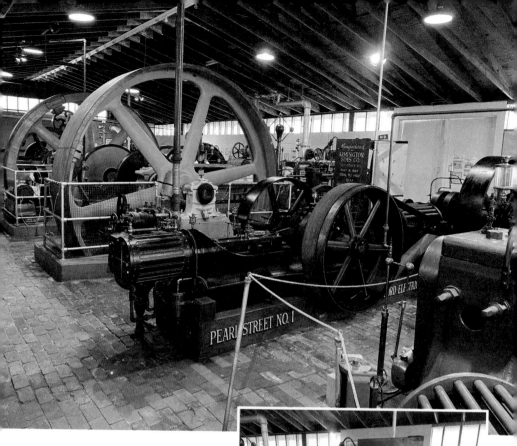

Operational steam engines at the New England Wireless & Steam Museum

housed in historic buildings in a pastoral section of East Greenwich and is open to the public on Saturday afternoons in the summer, but the best time to visit is during the annual Yankee Steam-Up in October, when the museum sets its engines in motion amid a cacophony of noise and smoke.

SACRED SACHEM

What famous Native American chief is buried behind the outfield of a Warren baseball field?

If you enjoy feasting at Thanksgiving, you can thank Massasoit, the great sachem of the Wampanoag tribe, who helped the Pilgrims fend off starvation in the early years of the Plymouth Colony. Ruling from his home village of Sowams, now part of Warren, Massasoit chiefly was responsible for the good relationship between the tribe and the European newcomers.

When he died in the 1660s, Massasoit was buried in a tribal cemetery on Burr's Hill in Warren, where his remains lay undisturbed until 1891, when the graveyard was unceremoniously pulled apart and looted during construction of the Old Colony Railroad. An amateur archaeologist disinterred the remaining graves and gave the remains and artifacts to Brown University and the Museum of the American Indian in New York.

BURR'S HILL PARK

WHAT: Massasoit Burial Site

WHERE: Burr's Hill Park, 540 Water St., Warren

COST: Free

PRO TIP: The park is adjacent to the East Bay Bike Path, a 13.8-mile rail trail built on the bed of the former Old Colony Railroad.

Massasoit maintained largely peaceful relations with European settlers during his life, but his son, Metacomet, led Native American forces in the bloody conflict that bore his Christian name: King Philip's War.

Left: Massasoit meets Massachusetts Governor John Carver

Right: Massasoit grave marker

One particular grave contained muskets, a war bonnet, and—crucially—a roll of gold lace matching that given to Massasoit by Plymouth Colony Governor Edward Winslow. Experts concluded that these were, indeed, the remains of the great sachem.

In 2017, Massasoit returned home when he was ceremonially reburied on Burr's Hill, in a grave facing the sunset in accordance with tribal tradition. Other artifacts from the cemetery also were reburied at the site, which is topped with a stone marker that reads, in part: "While memories of this land spark the fire of his spirit, let the smoke rise in prayerful respect to [Massasoit] . . . esteemed leader of the Wampanoag Nation. His vision and 1621 treaty upheld 54 years of peace with early English settlers." You can find the monument in the north end of Burr's Hill Park, just beyond the baseball field and adjacent to the Warren Town Beach.

GHOSTS OF GREBLE

Where can you paddle to the site of a former colonial trading post, Civil War fort, and POW camp in Narragansett Bay?

Dutch Island's name hearkens back to its earliest recorded history, when the Dutch West India Company set up a trading post in 1624 to trade with the Narragansett tribe, who called the island Quotenis. During the US Civil War, the strategically located island off the southwest coast of Conanicut Island (Jamestown) was the site of a coastal defense battery manned by a regiment of African American artillery soldiers, and during the Spanish–American War the bay's defenses were reinforced by the construction of Fort Greble.

The fort was equipped with batteries of heavy guns and mortars, though its soldiers never fired a shot in anger. By World War II, the guns had been removed and the fort served as a camp for German prisoners of war. Military use of the island waned after the war, and Fort Greble was gradually overgrown, with Dutch Island now mostly home to deer.

But the decaying remains of Fort Greble's concrete bunkers, buildings, dock, and roads remain on Dutch Island, along with the historic Dutch Island Light (built in 1857 and still operational). And it's all just a tantalizingly short paddle away from Jamestown's Dutch Harbor marina or Fort Getty. A kayak or small boat is currently the only way to reach the island, which is owned by the state of Rhode Island. A recent

DUTCH ISLAND

WHAT: Ruins of Fort Greble

WHERE: Dutch Island in Narragansett Bay

COST: Free

PRO TIP: The interior of the island is overgrown, but some of the old structures can be seen from the water or the beach.

Dutch Island lighthouse and abandoned buildings

cleanup by the military has made some of the ruins a little less hazardous, but exploring can still be dangerous, so the island remains officially off-limits to the public.

HAUNTED MANSION

Which Newport mansion was moved brick by brick from Washington, DC?

The Bay Voyage Hotel in Jamestown is named for the fact that it was cut in half and moved by boat in 1890 from Middletown to its present location. But that was a walk in the park compared to the journey undertaken by Newport's Seaview Terrace mansion in the 1920s.

The French Renaissance mansion began its storied life on Dupont Circle in Washington, DC, where it was built in 1876. Owned for decades by telephone inventor Alexander Graham Bell, the mansion was sold to distillery owner Edson Bradley in 1907. Bradley doubled the size of the home, to the point that it took up an entire District of Columbia city block and was dubbed Aladdin's Castle.

In 1925, however, Bradley and his wife decided to move to Newport . . . and take the mansion with them. At a cost of $2 million, the entire building was disassembled, loaded on trucks and trains, and moved north to be rebuilt on the Cliff Walk, joining the other sumptuous homes lining nearby Bellevue Avenue.

SEAVIEW TERRACE

WHAT: Relocated Newport mansion that became a movie star

WHERE: 207 Ruggles Ave., Newport

COST: None

PRO TIP: The house is private property, but you can get a glimpse of the exterior by peeking through the hedges surrounding the estate.

The property already had an Elizabethan Revival mansion called Sea View, but rather than tear it down, the owners simply incorporated the existing house into the relocated estate.

At 40,000 square feet and including a Gothic chapel, turrets, ballroom, and theater, Seaview Terrace is the fifth-

Seaview Terrace mansion (seaviewterrace.org)

largest Gilded Age mansion in Newport, and there are reportedly a number of ghosts rattling around the hallways. Maybe that's why the exterior of the mansion stood in for Collinwood Manor, the site of the popular Gothic soap opera *Dark Shadows*, which aired on ABC from 1966 to 1971 and still has a cult following.

Rhode Island has many houses said to be haunted, perhaps none more famous than the Old Arnold Estate in Harrisville, more popularly known as the Conjuring House.

DARK SKIES

Where can you search the stars with a 145-year-old telescope?

A telescope given to Frank Evans Seagrave for his 16th birthday in 1876 is the centerpiece of the Seagrave Memorial Observatory, located in the dark woods of North Scituate and a beacon for stargazers.

The observatory and Seagrave's 8¼-inch Alvan Clark refracting telescope originally were on Benefit Street in Providence, but growing air and light pollution in the city prompted the amateur astronomer to move the observatory to a treeless plateau in western Rhode Island. Seagrave made several contributions to astronomical science during his life, including correctly predicting Halley's Comet's location in 1910 and foretelling a total solar eclipse in New England in 1932.

When Seagrave died in 1934, he gifted the observatory and his beloved telescope to the Skyscrapers, the amateur astronomical society that has operated the facility ever since. Beginning in 1937, the Skyscrapers have invited the public to the Seagrave Memorial Observatory on Saturday nights to view the stars, planets, and other celestial bodies, as well as for special events like eclipses and meteor showers.

In addition to Seagrave's original telescope, the nonprofit membership organization also has a 12-inch Patton reflector

SEAGRAVE MEMORIAL OBSERVATORY

WHAT: Stargazing at a country estate

WHERE: 47 Peep Toad Rd., Scituate

COST: Free weekly public open houses

PRO TIP: Charlestown's Ninigret Park is one of the darkest spots on the East Coast, and its Frosty Drew Observatory also hosts public sky-gazing events.

The Seagrave Memorial Observatory

telescope and 12- and 16-inch computerized Meade Schmidt-Cassegrain telescopes. The 19th-century Seagrave telescope is mounted in the original observatory building, while a bigger observatory with a roll-off roof was constructed by club members to accommodate the newer telescopes.

The Skyscrapers' annual AstroAssembly convention attracts top astronomers, astrophysicists, scientists, and astronauts from around the world as speakers.

CLOSED MENU

What's the most tantalizing museum that you can't visit in Rhode Island?

If you're a fan of food, the Culinary Arts Museum at Johnson & Wales University in Providence is a smorgasbord of tasty treats, with a 250,000-item collection that includes ancient cooking utensils, stoves, and kitchen gear, thousands of restaurant menus dating back as far as the 1500s, and an entire art deco diner dating from the 1920s—a special nod to Rhode Island's status as the birthplace of these mobile eateries.

Yet it's all as near and yet far away as peering at pastries in a bakery window after hours, because the museum, opened in 1989, stopped admitting the public in 2017. The Culinary Arts Museum still exists, but it's now open only to Johnson & Wales students, teachers, alumni, and visiting researchers.

JOHNSON & WALES UNIVERSITY CULINARY ARTS MUSEUM

WHAT: Museum devoted to food, cooking, and restaurants

WHERE: 315 Harborside Blvd., Providence

COST: Free, but not open to the general public

PRO TIP: Many of Rhode Island's top restaurants are helmed by Johnson & Wales graduates, including Champ Speidel at Persimmon, Ben Sukle of Oberlin, and Derek Wagner of Nick's on Broadway.

Restaurant chef was long considered a profession primarily for men, but Johnson & Wales University was founded by—and named for—two women, Gertrude Johnson and Mary Wales.

Culinary museum exhibits (Johnson & Wales University)

Located at the culinary and hospitality school's Harborside Campus, the museum galleries are used as one of the coolest college study halls around. Visitors who do manage to get in can congregate for work or play on a re-created country fair midway, bathe in the light of vintage neon restaurant signs, and peruse display cases full of old cookbooks, cake molds, and other eating ephemera.

However, the public isn't entirely shut off from such tidbits as what was for lunch on the SS *Arabic* cruise ship on September 3, 1927 (split pea soup, codfish steak meunière, spring carrots, and mousseline potatoes), or that the Bay State Hotel served up sirloin steak with béarnaise sauce for 90 cents a plate back in 1886. The school is in process of digitizing the museum's entire collection in order to make it available online.

161

ROTTEN TOMATOES

What Newport painter got Americans to eat "deadly" tomatoes?

There was a time when the tomato, now commonly found topping pizza, pasta, and salads, was considered exotic in America. Not just strange, but poisonous. The belief in the tomato's toxicity persisted into the mid-19th century, until its plum reputation was rehabilitated by an artist who had emigrated from Europe to Newport.

The plaque on the side of Michel Felice Cornè's house in Newport declares that the Italian-born nautical painter, who came to the City by the Sea in 1822, "introduced the tomato into this country." And while that's not exactly accurate—tomatoes can be found in early colonial recipes, and Thomas Jefferson was said to be a tomato aficionado—Cornè did help disabuse New Englanders of their notion that the so-called "love apple" would induce madness or suicide.

The idea isn't as off-base as you might think. The tomato is a member of the nightshade family, some of which, like belladonna, are poisonous. Cornè didn't launch some grand educational or propaganda campaign in favor of the tomato: he just assured his friends and neighbors of the tomato's safety by eating them every day without dropping dead or jumping off the steeple of Trinity Church. In something of a Catch-22, some of Cornè's neighbors thought him insane simply because of his

MICHEL FELICE CORNÈ HOUSE

WHAT: Cornè tomato house

WHERE: 2 Corne St., Newport

COST: Free to view, but the house—which has a tomato-red front door—is not open to the public.

PRO TIP: Newport's Redwood Library has a self-portrait of Cornè on display.

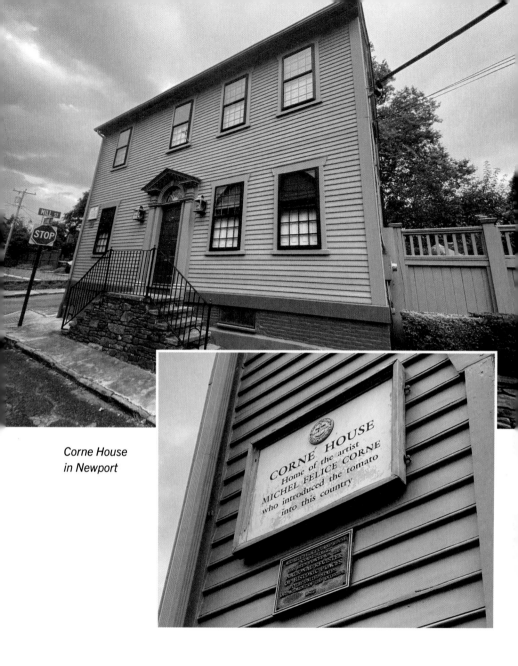

*Corne House
in Newport*

eating habits, but the artist went so far as to consume an entire bag of tomatoes in public to convince Newporters that their lives would be far richer in a world filled with caprese salad and pico de gallo.

RUNES OF THE DAY

Did Vikings carve a mysterious stone found in the waters of Narragansett Bay?

Under a gazebo in the village of Wickford sits a rock, and while it's no Plymouth Rock, it's actually far more interesting than that gimmicky stone in Massachusetts. Because, while the "1620" carved on the spot where the Pilgrims supposedly landed actually dates only to 1880, the mysterious markings on the Narragansett Rune Stone may have been left by Viking explorers.

Or not. The truth is that nobody knows what the Rune Stone markings are, or how they got there. What is known is this: the 2.5-ton boulder, also known as the Quidnessett Rock, originally was located in the waters of Narragansett Bay, just offshore from Pojac Point in North Kingstown.

Familiar to local children from the 1940s on as "Indian Rock," the stone became more widely known in the 1980s after a quahogger reported seeing two rows of what appeared to be Nordic runes carved into its side.

Then, the rock disappeared, possibly excavated by a nearby property owner fed up with curiosity-seekers invading his property. The rock allegedly even served as the base of a glass-topped coffee table for a time before being retrieved by authorities.

OLD LIBRARY PARK

WHAT: Narragansett Rune Stone

WHERE: 55 Brown St., North Kingstown

COST: Free

PRO TIP: If you love tales about Leif Erikson, be sure to also check out the Viking Tower in Newport, which probably is a mill built in the 17th century but also just might be an ancient Norse church.

The Narragansett Rune Stone

In 2015, however, the Narragansett Rune Stone found a new—and hopefully permanent—home in downtown Wickford. The runes never have been translated, nor the rock examined scientifically, so it's anyone's guess who carved the stone—Vikings? Indians? The Knights Templar? A couple of teenagers from Providence? But at least now you can speculate while viewing it in one of Rhode Island's prettiest colonial villages, instead of having to wade into the bay.

The Narragansett Rune Stone is made of sandstone, making it relatively easy to carve.

RACE TRACES

How did Pawtucket become a pit stop for New England auto racing fans?

Rhode Island doesn't have a single auto racing track—the closest is in Seekonk, Massachusetts—which makes it an unusual place to have a motorsports museum. But the state once was a hotbed of stock car racing, boasting nine tracks at one point, and the ProNyne Motorsports Museum does its best to keep those memories alive.

Founded by race fans Robert Silvia and Ric Mariscal, the 7,400-square-foot museum is jammed with racing memorabilia, from track advertisements and programs to helmets, photos, and trophies. The crown jewels, however, are the 15 vintage race cars on display, including Ford Pintos and Vegas modified for racing. Many of the cars once raced on long-vanished Rhode Island tracks like the Lonsdale Sports Arena and the Tiverton Speedway, but one that didn't is a yellow, No. 4, Kodak Winston Cup Oldsmobile—that car was driven by Tom Cruise in the 1990 film *Days of Thunder*.

Rhode Island had a small but significant place in racing history: the first auto race on an oval track was held in Cranston in 1896, and Rhode Island native Fred Desarro was the National

PRONYNE MOTORSPORTS MUSEUM

WHAT: Collection of stock cars and racing memorabilia

WHERE: 8 Cleveland St., Pawtucket

COST: Free; donations welcome

PRO TIP: The Modern Diner, right around the corner from the museum on East Ave., is the kind of joint where you'd run into race car drivers back in the day. Built in 1940, it's the only Sterling Streamliner diner still in operation—designed after a locomotive, not a race car, alas.

Stock cars in the ProNyne Motorsports Museum

Association for Stock Car Racing (NASCAR) National Modified Champion in 1970. The state's auto racing tracks are all gone now, but the golden age of racing in Rhode Island lives on in Pawtucket, where the museum still gets some love from race fans attending events at the Seekonk Speedway a few miles away.

The Seekonk Speedway has been hosting races since 1946, when it opened on land that previously had been a poultry farm.

MONSTER MEETUPS

Why does a merry troupe of monsters roam the streets of Providence?

If you happen to encounter a party of aliens and robots in Providence's Kennedy Plaza or Burnside Park, don't be alarmed. It's probably not a Martian invasion, but rather an appearance by Big Nazo.

BIG NAZO LAB

WHAT: Big Nazo creature encounters

WHERE: City streets and the lab at 1386 Westminster St., Providence

COST: Free; donations welcome

PRO TIP: Big Nazo creatures make 3–4 random appearances weekly, with Kennedy Plaza the most likely place to have an encounter.

For more than three decades, this group of Providence-based performance artists has been building a collection of freakishly oversized "puppet creatures" that make random appearances on city streets, as well as take part in events like PVD Fest, WaterFire, and the city's annual St. Patrick's Day parade. Hop on a trolley for Providence's monthly gallery night, and there might be a giant talking dog puppet in the seat next to you. Walk across the new pedestrian bridge spanning the Providence River, and you could be joined by a fleet of "Strollbots."

And if you're lucky, you'll get a glimpse of Quasimodo, the "founding father" of Big Nazo, who has been regarding passersby with his three googly eyes for more than 30 years.

Big Nazo puppets can also occasionally be seen performing as the Big Nazo Intergalactic Creature Band, playing mostly rock and funk music.

Big Nazo Strollbots (Big Nazo Lab)

Big Nazo has appeared around the world but remains firmly rooted to Providence. In addition to spontaneous meetups on downtown streets and during festivals, you can commune with the characters at the group's new headquarters in the city's West End neighborhood. Some of the 1,000-plus creatures in storage stare out from windows in the two-story building, and visitors also are welcomed into the fabrication shop to see how the puppets are made, and perhaps to touch and try on some creature heads and costumes, too.

RUST NEVER SLEEPS

Why is a prime strip of coastal Rhode Island filled with rusty junk?

We all know that water causes metal to rust, and nothing causes corrosion quite as quickly as seawater. That's why, for decades, the aluminum company Alcoa has placed samples of all sorts of products, from nuts and bolts to window frames and aircraft parts, on racks facing the ocean in Narragansett and let nature do its worst.

The Point Judith Corrosion Test Facility, located on a one-acre plot of land adjacent to the much more prominent Point Judith Lighthouse, has been quietly measuring the resistance of aluminum products to salty mist and rain since the 1920s. Some of the materials at the site literally have been slowly rusting away—or not, because aluminum doesn't actually rust, although it can corrode—for decades.

The 70 or so racks of test materials run from the end of State Route 108 right down to the beach. The site is closed to

Saltwater corrodes metal five times faster than fresh water due to its sodium chlorine content, and salty, humid air is 10 times more corrosive than air with normal humidity.

Racks of materials being tested at the Point Judith Corrosion Test Facility

the public, but can easily be viewed through a chain-link fence. It's not much to look at, but information gathered here is used by the military, as well as company researchers. The value of the Point Judith Corrosion Test Facility can best be surmised by the location. Why else would you site a glorified junk pile on a beautiful sliver of Rhode Island beachfront with a million-dollar view?

ROYAL REFUGE

Where is a rare stone fort built by the Narragansett tribe for its queen located?

Battles between Europeans and Native Americans in North America often are portrayed as hit-and-run affairs, but in truth both sides built and attacked fortified defensive positions raised by their adversaries. In King Philip's War, for example, the Great Swamp Massacre in 1675 involved an attack by Massachusetts militia against a Narragansett fort surrounded by wooden stockade walls. The Narragansetts' Queen's Fort in Exeter, however, was unique because it featured well-constructed stone walls, a feature far more common to European defenses.

The Queen's Fort was a product of King Philip's War, which initially pitted the Massachusetts Bay Colony against the Wampanoag tribe, but eventually drew in the neutral Narragansetts, too.

After the Great Swamp Massacre, Narragansett Queen Quaiapen and some of her people sought refuge in the forests of Exeter. Stonewall John, a Narragansett man who had learned stonemasonry from the English, oversaw construction of a hilltop fortification, building stone walls between glacial boulders to protect the queen from attacks by raiding English militia. Sadly, the queen was persuaded to leave the fort's

Hilltop redoubt at the Queen's Fort in Exeter

defenses, and in 1676 she, Stonewall John, and many of her people were ambushed and killed in a battle at Mattity Swamp in North Smithfield.

The fort, however, has survived. At first glance, it looks like so many of the old stone walls built at the edges of farmers' fields in New England. But its strategic location is obvious from the top of the hill, and visitors can only wonder how long the Narragansetts could have held out here if they had remained.

MURDER MEMORIAL

Why was the murder of William Jackson at a crossroads in South Kingstown memorialized in stone?

The 18th-century murder of William Jackson on Tower Hill in South Kingstown was a textbook example of "stranger danger" that has stood the test of time and the elements. Jackson, by all accounts, was a mensch: a trader of animal skins, he was on the road to Boston when he met Thomas Carter of Newport, a sea captain who had recently been shipwrecked in North Carolina and was making his way home. Jackson reportedly shared money and his horse with Carter, and the two spent a night in a South County inn together.

For reasons that aren't entirely clear, things between the two men took a dark turn around midnight on the night of January 1, 1751, when Carter attacked Jackson, killing him, taking his money, and throwing his body into the Narrow River. After the corpse was found, an innkeeper recognized Jackson as a recent guest who had been accompanied by Carter. The murderous captain was captured in Newport, tried, convicted of Jackson's murder, and publicly executed. His body hung in chains near the

Carter Jackson Monument

intersection of Post Road (US Route 1) and Torrey Road long after his death, as a warning to other wannabe highwaymen.

The story of the murder, and tales of hearing rattling chains from Carter's gibbet, remained part of local lore for more than a century before Joseph Peace Hazard, a prominent local resident and spiritualist, erected a monument to Jackson at the site of his murder. The four-foot granite monument, which dates from 1889, offers an account of the events surrounding Jackson's death and Carter's execution, the story carved on all four sides of the pillar.

SOURCES

Mo' Nukes
Personal visit; New England
Historical Society; *Yankee* magazine
(newengland.com/today/living/new-
england-history/nuclear-accident-
at-wood-river-junction), ecori.org/
smart-growth/2016/1/5/tragic-death-
gives-way-to-reborn-environment.

Rail Tales
Personal visit; artinruins.com/
property/east-side-train-tunnel;
ripta.com/tunnel.

Bridge to the Future
Personal visit; lostnewengland.
com/2016/11/crawford-street-bridge-
providence-ri.

Burnside's Sideburns
history.com/topics/american-civil-
war/ambrose-everett-burnside;
allthatsinteresting.com/ambrose-
burnside-sideburns.

Stalag South County
Personal visit; smallstatebighistory.
com/the-top-secret-world-war-ii-
prisoner-of-war-camp-at-fort-kearney-
in-narragansett.

Shopping Shafts
Personal visit; gardencitycenter.
com; smallstatebighistory.com/how-
curious-a-coal-mine-in-cranston;
rimonthly.com/garden-citys-past-and-
present.

Lost Island
warwickonline.com/stories/the-island-
that-disappeared,151976.

Tara North
Personal visit; stories.
usatodaynetwork.com/
slaveryinrhodeisland/plantations-
in-the-north-the-narragansett-
planters; smallstatebighistory.com/
narragansett-planters-commercial-
agriculture-colonial-south-county;

newenglandhistoricalsociety.com/
hannah-robinson-tragic-love-affair-
unfortunate.

Strange Endeavor
nhm.ac.uk/discover/hms-
endeavour-250.html; livescience.
com/captain-cook-endeavour-
shipwreck-possibly-discovered.html;
arstechnica.com/science/2018/09/
captain-cooks-hms-endeavour-found-
off-the-coast-ofrhode-island.

Yo Ho, Oh No
Personal visit;
newenglandhistoricalsociety.com/
the-day-rhode-island-hanged-26-
pirates; rimonthly.com/newport-and-
its-pirates-a-love-hate-relationship;
smallstatebighistory.com/twenty-six-
pirates-hanged-at-newport.

Classical Gas
Personal visit; atlasobscura.com/
places/location-of-the-first-gas-street-
lamp; newporthistory.org/history-
bytes-gas-lighting-in-newport.

Welcome Cone
Personal visit; wpri.com/news/water-
cooler/pineapple-or-pine-cone-a-
look-at-the-federal-hill-arch-debate;
federalhillprov.com/about/lapigna-the-
pineapple.

Look, Up in the Sky . . .
Personal visit; ppsri.org/
advocacy/current-advocacy/
industrial-trust-superman-
building; providencejournal.
com/story/news/2019/05/29/
providences-superman-building-
listed-as-one-of-nations-most-
endangeredplaces/5029612007;
sah-archipedia.org/buildings/RI-01-
PR3.

Mighty 'Mite
Personal visit; roadsideamerica.
com/story/11598; bigbluebug.com/
the-big-blue-bug; entnemdept.ufl.
edu/creatures/urban/termites/native_
subterraneans.htm.

Rolling to Victory
Personal visit; pro-football-reference.
com/teams/prv;goldenrankings.
com/providencesteamroller.
htm; sportsecyclopedia.com/nfl/
providence/steamroller.html.

Little High Point
Personal visit; alltrails.com/trail/us/
rhode-island/jerimoth-hill-rhode-
island-highpoint; summitpost.org/
jerimoth-hill/152342.

Red Royalty
Personal visit; chickensandmore.com/
rhode-island-red; backyardpoultry.
iamcountryside.com/chickens-101/
the-history-of-rhode-island-red-
chickens; rimonthly.com/little-
compton-and-the-rhode-island-red-a-
history.

Soldier Snatching
Personal visit; tivertonhistory.
wordpress.com/american-
revolution/lt-colonel-william-barton;
newenglandhistoricalsociety.com/
british-general-richard-prescott-gets-
evicted-summer-home.

Historic Roots
Personal visit; nps.gov/rowi/learn/
news/the-tree-root-that-ate-roger-
williams.htm; rihs.org/the-root-of-the-
matter.

Urban Surf
Personal visit; info.risd.edu/
tillinghast-place; instagram.com/p/
BoNAClhAqVN/?hl=en; tftmmelrose.
com/product/daybreak-bronze-
sculpture-gilbert-franklin.

Princely Pup
Personal visit; rwpconservancy.
org/sentinel; cool.culturalheritage.
org/byorg/hp/PROGRAMS/
SOS/4KIDS/4kids2000/RISentinel.htm;
golocalprov.com/news/brown-selling-
mansion-for-2.5m-links-to-moses-
brown-richest-woman-in-americ.

An Elephant Never Forgets
Personal visit; chepachet.com/betty.
htm; smallstatebighistory.com/an-
elephant-is-murdered-in-chepachet-
in-1826.

Busy Bee
Personal visit; seabeemuseum.
wordpress.com/2015/03/05/curators-
corner-the-birth-of-the-fighting-bee.

Elusive Headstones
Personal visit; tourosynagogue.
org/history/jewish-burial-ground;
whatsupnewp.com/2020/08/public-
invited-to-visit-colonial-jewish-
cemetery-on-august-16.

White (Pasta) Riot
Personal visit; smallstatebighistory.
com/providence-macaroni-riots-1914;
rhodetour.org/items/show/152;
newenglandhistoricalsociety.com/
pasta-la-vista-f-p-ventrone-sparks-
providence-macaroni-riots.

Kicked Can
Personal visit; artinruins.com/
property/milk-can; quahog.org/
Attractions/Big_Milk_Can.

Superficial Reading
Personal visit; atlasobscura.
com/places/john-hay-library-0;
browndailyherald.com/
article/2021/10/what-the-hay-
hides-exploring-the-special-
collections; biblio.com/blog/2019/10/
anthropodermic-bibliopegy-books-
bound-in-human-skin.

Dread Head
Personal visit; brown.edu/cis/sta/dev/
providence_architecture/locations/
downtown/turks_head_building;
guide.ppsri.org/property/turks-head-
building; atlasobscura.com/places/
turks-head-building.

Gag Order
Personal visit;
olneyvillenewyorksystem.com/about.

Magnetic Mystery Rocks
Personal visit; roadsideamerica.
com/tip/43873; geocaching.com/
geocache/GC51DR2_only-in-rhode-
island.

Hung, Drawn, and Quartered
Personal visit; quahog.org/
FactsFolklore/Personalities/Tefft_
Joshua_Execution.

A Whale of a Sad Tale
Personal visit; newenglandlighthouses.
net/whale-rock-light-history.html;
rhodeislandlighthousehistory.info/
whale_rock_lighthouse.html.

Nine Men's Misery
Personal visit; newengland.com/
today/travel/rhode-island/nine-mens-
misery-historic-site-in-cumberland-ri;
newenglandhistoricalsociety.com/
nine-mens-misery-oldest-veterans-
memorial-honors-tortured-plymouth-
colonists.

Reach the Beaches
Personal visit; independentri.com/
southcountylifemagazine/inside_the_
magazine/features/article_6a0ee958-
f3bb-5449-a1db-ce3387453bc7.
html; quonset.com/about-the-park/
amenities/four-public-beaches/
default.aspx.

Swamp Span
Personal visit; sites.google.com/site/
harrysbridges/home/rhode-island-
covered-bridges.

Watery Graves
Personal visit; scituateri.net/qrtour/
Reservoir.htm; johnstonsunrise.net/
stories/submerged-but-not-forgotten-
the-lost-villages-of-scituate,49637;
rimonthly.com/the-secrets-of-
scituate-reservoir.

Wat's Up, Buddha?
Personal visit; quahog.org/Attractions/
Angkor_Wat_Replica.

Funky Fleur
Personal visit; providenceartclub.org/
about/our-buildings/the-fleur-de-lys-
building; guide.ppsri.org/property/
fleur-de-lys-studios.

Giving Props
US Naval War College; oceanexplorer.
noaa.gov/technology/development-
partnerships/18kraken/u853-
blackpoint/u853-blackpoint.html;
smallstatebighistory.com/german-u-
boat-u-853-stripped-of-some-of-its-
major-artifacts.

Stars in the Bucket
Personal visit; roadsideamerica.
com/tip/44973; film.ri.gov/
FilmOfficeEvents/WoodyPawtucket.
html; post-gazette.com/ae/
movies/2014/08/09/Woody-Allen-s-
handprints-on-Pawtucket-walk-of-
fame/stories/201408090032?print=1.

Cemetery Carvers
Personal visit; johnstevensshop.com;
ripnewport.com/carvers.html.

Nazi Pup
Personal visit; World War II Foundation
Museum; express.co.uk/news/
world/1366051/adolf-hitler-dog-
blondi-eva-braun-berlin-bunker-
death-cyanide-soviet-unionworld-war-
2-spt; medium.com/short-history/
hitlers-favourite-dog-1cfc8f047924.

Creamy Cabinets
Personal visit; npr.org/sections/
thesalt/2016/09/05/492278535/
whats-in-that-coffee-cabinet-a-
delicious-taste-of-rhode-islandhistory;
eater.com/2016/9/8/12835908/
coffee-cabinet-rhode-island;
rimonthly.com/history-delektas-
pharmacy.

Partitioned Prudence
Personal visit; kids.kiddle.co/
Prudence_Island; newportri.com/
story/lifestyle/2021/07/06/prudence-
island-offers-hiking-bicycling-and-
a-fungetaway-near-newport-rhode-
island/7689081002; rimonthly.com/
narragansett-bay-islands.

Black Diamond
Personal visit; newenglandskihistory.
com/RhodeIsland/diamondhill.
php; newenglandskihistory.com/
RhodeIsland/skivalley.php.

Plucked Cluck
Personal visit; rimonthly.com/behind-the-scenes-savoring-federal-hill.

Cloistered Cookies
Personal visit, Wright's Dairy Farm; bonappetit.com/story/hermit-cookie-reclusive-recipe.

A Whole Lotta Lotus
Personal visit; independentri.com/independents/north_east/opinion/article_a0b0f1d1-a52d-5f6f-8d51-cf40a957bc7f.html.

Robert the Hermit
hermitary.com/articles/robert.html.

Secret Spray
Personal visit; smallstatebighistory.com/beavertails-top-secret-spraycliff-observatory-world-war-ii; christianmcburney.com/portfolio-items/untold-stories-from-world-war-ii-rhode-island.

Elite Animals
Personal research; oceanhourfarm.org

The Unforgettable Fire
Personal visit; cbsnews.com/news/the-station-nightclub-fire-rhode-island-what-happened-and-whos-to-blame; thestationfirememorialfoundation.org; nbcnews.com/news/us-news/memorialpark-opens-site-rhode-island-nightclub-fire-killed-100-n762736.

Egg Rolls and Jazz
Personal visit; chanseggrollsandjazz.com; providencejournal.com/story/entertainment/dining/2021/12/03/eggrolls-and-jazz-restaurantand-jazz-club-chans-sale-in-woonsocket/8734569002.

Mall Rats
providencejournal.com/story/news/2018/02/17/where-are-theynow-artist-wishes-he-could-go-home-again-to-providence-place-mall/14440148007; wrafwraf.com/trummerkind.html; 99percentinvisible.org/episode/the-accidental-room.

Shots through the Dorr
Personal visit; newengland.com/today/living/new-englandhistory/dorr-rebellion; newenglandhistoricalsociety.com/dorr-rebellion-ri-2-governors.

Animal Art
The Rhode Island School of Design, naturelab.risd.edu.

The Battle of Rhode Island
Personal visit; revolutionarywar.us/year-1778/battle-rhode-island.

Horse Soldiers
Personal visit; artinruins.com/property/narragansett-race-track; townandcountrymag.com/leisure/sporting/a10000879/narragansett-parkracetrack-war.

Civic Suds
Personal visit; narragansettbeer.com/our-story; independentri.com/independents/south_county/narragansett/article_7f44a3cb-5fc1-5434-9279-c6d68af4bac9.html.

Punked Procession
Town of Chepachet; glocesterri.org/parade.htm; destinationeatdrink.medium.com/ancients-horribles-parade-17d88eeb251.

Yankee Doodle Daddy
Personal visit; songhall.org/profile/George_M_Cohan; irishamerica.com/2011/12/providence-gives-regards-to-cohan.

The Pirates Retirement Home
warwickonline.com/stories/a-glimpse-of-ris-pastcaptain-thomas-paine-of-jamestown,1766; jamestownpress.com/articles/paine-went-from-high-seas-to-early-jamestown-settler.

Family Guy
rhodetour.org/items/show/164; familyguy.fandom.com/wiki/Quahog,_Rhode_Island.

A Tree Grows in Bristol
Personal visit, Blithewold
Mansion, Gardens and Arboretum;
finegardening.com/article/the-tallest-
redwood-east-of-the-rockies.

Clinging Shingles
nytimes.com/2008/08/07/
garden/07clingstone.html;
sightsailing.com/uncategorized/
blog-clingstone; blog.dockwa.com/
narragansett-bays-house-on-a-rock-a-
look-inside-clingstone.

Troubled Temple
Personal visit; guide.ppsri.org/
property/masonic-temple; artinruins.
com/property/masonic-temple-pvd.

Bad Boys
Personal visit; artinruins.com/
property/sockanosset-boys-
school; rhodetour.org/items/
show/29?tour=1&index=7.

Game Room with a View
Personal visit; springlakearcade.com/
homepage.html; atlasobscura.com/
places/spring-lake-arcade.

Bus Line
Personal visit; smallstatebighistory.
com/sea-rail-narragansett-pier-
railroad; traillink.com/trail/william-c-
oneill-bike-path.

Hot Potatoes
Personal visit; onlyinyourstate.com/
rhode-island/mr-potato-heads-ri;
chowdaheadz.com/blogs/news/take-
a-mr-potato-head-themed-rhode-trip-
across-rhode-island.

Avenue Arts
Personal visit; theavenueconcept.org;
artculturetourism.com/public-art-tour.

French Frescoes
rimonthly.com/inside-st-anns-in-
woonsocket-the-sistine-chapel-of-new-
england; newenglandhistoricalsociety.
com/the-40-angels-st-ann-the-sistine-
chapel-of-woonsocket.

Hobbit Houses
Personal visit; Paul Mihailides,
preservesportingclub.com.

Head Shot
Personal visit; findagrave.com/
memorial/28863455/john-
rogersvinton.

Fired-Up Farm
Personal visit; newsm.org.

Sacred Sachem
Personal visit; smithsonianmag.
com/smart-news/massasoitchief-
who-signed-treaty-pilgrims-
be-reburied-180962928;
sowamsheritagearea.org/wp/burrs-
hill-burial-ground.

Ghosts of Greble
Personal visit; golocalprov.com/
news/The-Allure-and-Dangers-of-
Jamestowns-Dutch-Island; rhodetour.
org/items/show/291.

Haunted Mansion
Personal visit; loveproperty.com/
gallerylist/133649/seaview-terrace-
tour-the-29m-rhode-island-mansion-
moved-400-miles; dupontcastle.com/
castles/seaviewt.htm; whatsupnewp.
com/2021/06/on-this-day-in-history-
june-27-1966-dark-shadows-
premieres-on-abc-carey-mansion-
used-as-collinwood-mansion.

Dark Skies
Personal visit; theskyscrapers.org;
cs.astronomy.com/asy/b/astronomy/
archive/2014/07/22/guest-blog-
seagrave-memorial-observatory-
centennial-1914-2014.aspx.

Closed Menu
Johnson & Wales Culinary Arts
Museum, jwu.edu/culinarymuseum.

Rotten Tomatoes
Personal visit; hellenicaworld.com/
Art/Paintings/en/MicheleFeliceCorne.
html; atlasobscura.com/places/corne-
house.

Runes of the Day

Personal visit; independentri.com/independents/ind/north_kingstown/article_59f859ac-dfa7-5a46-8072-1c4e1fc12a52.html; sorhodeisland.com/stories/the-great-narragansett-rune-stone-debate,17149.

Race Traces

ProNyne Motorsports Museum, nerferscornerreloaded.wordpress.com/the-pronyne-motorsports-museum.

Monster Meetups

bignazo.com.

Rust Never Sleeps

Personal visit; clui.org/ludb/site/seacoast-weathering-station-point-judith; roadsideamerica.com/story/2209.

Royal Refuge

Personal visit; smallstatebighistory.com/queens-fort-stone-refuge-for-quaiapen-1675-1676; trailsandwalksri.wordpress.com/2014/12/28/queens-fort-exeter.

Murder Memorial

Personal visit; hmdb.org/m.asp?m=29314; smallstatebighistory.com/jackson-murdered-carter-hanged-sure.

INDEX